MORE

PHILOSOPHY
FOR *TEENS*

MORE
PHILOSOPHY
FOR TEENS

EXAMINING REALITY AND KNOWLEDGE

SHARON M. KAYE, PH.D., & PAUL THOMSON, PH.D.

ILLUSTRATED BY JON COMPTON

PRUFROCK PRESS INC.
WACO, TX

Library of Congress Cataloging-in-Publication Data

Kaye, Sharon M.
  More philosophy for teens : examining reality and knowledge / Sharon M. Kaye and Paul Thomson.
     p. cm.
  Includes bibliographical references.
  ISBN-13: 978-1-59363-292-2 (pbk.)
  ISBN-10: 1-59363-292-4 (pbk.)
  1. Philosophy. I. Thomson, Paul. II. Title.
  BD31.K283 2007
  100—dc22
                      2007027298

Copyright © 2008 Prufrock Press Inc.
Edited by Lacy Elwood
Cover and Layout Design by Marjorie Parker
Illustrations by Jon Compton

ISBN-13: 978-1-59363-292-2
ISBN-10: 1-59363-292-4

Printed in the United States of America.

At the time of this book's publication, all facts and figures cited are the most current available. All telephone numbers, addresses, and Web site URLs are accurate and active. All publications, organizations, Web sites, and other resources exist as described in the book, and all have been verified. The authors and Prufrock Press Inc., make no warranty or guarantee concerning the information and materials given out by organizations or content found at Web sites, and we re not responsible for any changes that occur after this book's publication. If you find an error, please contact Prufrock Press Inc.

Prufrock Press Inc.
P.O. Box 8813
Waco, TX 76714-8813
Phone: (800) 998-2208
Fax: (800) 240-0333
http://www.prufrock.com

For Tris and Robin with love

TABLE OF CONTENTS

PART 1: THE SELF

PART 2: KNOWLEDGE

PART 3: THE UNIVERSE

PART 4: GOD

THOUGHT EXPERIMENTS

FALLACY FILES

PREFACE

Welcome to *More Philosophy for Teens*, the second volume of our series teaching philosophical issues to teenagers. Although the first book focused on aesthetics and ethics, this volume focuses on epistemology and metaphysics. Like the first volume, it is arranged topically rather than historically in order to emphasize the connection between ideas. We have, however, included relevant historical details offset from the main text.

Each chapter opens with a casual and realistic dialogue between two fictional teenagers who disagree about something (e.g., over whether moral rules apply to everyone or about whether God exists). Their disagreement illustrates two philosophical positions on an issue, setting up the topic for the chapter. In each chapter we explore two or more sides of a classical philosophical debate. The debate always includes a "thought experiment" to test the more controversial claims. At the end of each chapter are reading comprehension questions, discussion questions, exercises, activities, and references for further reading. Our goal is to bring philosophy alive through active learning.

We hope you enjoy reading this book as much as we enjoyed writing it! Please feel free to contact us with comments and suggestions.

Sharon Kaye (skaye@jcu.edu)
Paul Thomson (paulthomson@columbiasecondary.org)

ACKNOWLEDGMENTS

This project began life as the textbook we use for teaching in the Carroll-Cleveland Philosophers' Program at John Carroll University in Cleveland, OH. This program brings students from the Cleveland Municipal School District to our campus once a week for a philosophy, service learning, and enrichment class. We are the co-directors of the program. Drafts of this book have been used in the program many times, and we think that this has resulted in a well-tested final product. We would like to thank all of the people who helped launch this project. There are too many to mention by name.

We give special thanks to: Dr. Jenifer Merritt, founder of the Carroll-Cleveland Philosophers' Program; municipal students and teachers who participated in the Carroll-Cleveland Philosophers' Program; Brittany McClane, Program Operations Director for 2006–2007; our John Carroll University undergraduate teaching assistants in the program—Dan Matusicky, Linda Kawentel, Rhiannon Lathy, Alex Decker, Marie Semple, and Betsy Rafferty; Domina Maria St. Catherine, secretary of our department; Marc Engel, Shaker Heights High School student, who proofed the penultimate draft and helped write the final chapter; Robert and Laurie Kaye for proofing early drafts; and our fellow faculty members.

We would also like to give special thanks to John Carroll University for research leave during the spring of 2006 and for its generous support of the Carroll-Cleveland Philosophers' Program.

TEACHER'S GUIDE

Although this book can be read on its own, it is especially useful in the classroom. We have implemented it with success in a wide variety of settings, from special classes with 50 teens and 10 teaching assistants, to standard classes with 25 teens and one teacher, to occasional workshops with 10 learners of different ages.

We have designed each chapter to teach itself in one session. Of course, ideally, the students would read the chapter on their own prior to class. Because the chapters are fun and accessible, this is a reasonable assignment. Nevertheless, we often proceed, and proceed fruitfully, without assigning any homework at all. When we have a 2-hour time block, a typical class period goes as follows: (1) we introduce the central question featured in the chapter; (2) we do a dramatic reading of the opening dialogue; (3) we write answers to the questions at the end of the dialogue; (4) we discuss highlights from the chapter (this may involve reading sections of text out loud together); (5) we write dialogues in small groups; (6) we perform the dialogues for the class and share our reactions. When we have just a one-hour time block we simply eliminate steps five and six or continue with those steps at the next class meeting. In courses that include steps five and six, we often make a video of the best dialogues for the students to watch together on the last day of class and, if copies can be made, to take home as a special memento.

Our students deeply enjoy the performance aspect of our "drama pedagogy"—to such an extent that dialogue production can begin to take over the class. The perennial issues discussed in each chapter have a way of fanning the flames of their creative energy! We recommend adhering to a schedule and keeping dialogues short to allow plenty of time to share reactions. We have developed a "dialogue worksheet" to facilitate this process. (Please see Appendix A at the back of this book.) The worksheet assigns clear roles to each of the students and brings the purpose of their performance into focus. Drama provides rare opportunities for self-transformation. Having witnessed these in our classroom time and again, we deem the effort well worth it.

The educational standards addressed by the book include history, English, and science. The exercises are designed to improve general literacy along with written and oral communication skills. The chapters need not be read in order, as the content of each is independent of the others. Teachers can make this book the basis for a full course in philosophy or introduce relevant chapters into other preexisting courses. For example, a history class studying the ancient world would benefit from Chapters 5 and 10, which feature Plato and Aristotle, respectively. Chapters 1 and 7 correspond to works of literature commonly studied in English classes. A science class would find value in Chapter 11, which discusses Albert Einstein; Chapter 12, which discusses Karl Popper; and Chapter 13, which discusses Richard Dawkins. Furthermore, any of the chapters would enhance dialogue work in a drama class. We have found the book to be highly adaptable to different learning environments, helping students think about old subjects in new ways.

This book enables teachers to assess students in multiple dimensions through written work, oral performance, and group projects. Because there are no right or wrong answers in philosophy, it can be a difficult subject to grade. In fact, the teacher's main responsibility is to encourage students to explore and be respectful of a wide variety of opinions. However, written work (whether this be answers to questions in the book or a running free-form philosophy journal) can be graded for excellence of expression. We recommend requiring the students to turn in some written work at the end of each class to receive written feedback whether with or without a grade. A point system for class participation may also be useful to reward quality contributions and cooperation. Students should come away from the course (or course unit) understanding the importance of clear thinking and communication. They will be excited to discover that human beings have been wondering about the same things they have for a very long time. In our experience, this excitement translates into leaps and bounds of learning.

INTRODUCTION

Do you ever think about weird things?

For example, have you ever been angry with your computer? Do you think that it could care about you being mad? Do you think we could build a machine that could care? Do you think we could build a machine that could think? What do you think "thinking" is?

Do you think that the universe had a beginning? If you do, what do you think went on before that? Do you think that you have been put on this Earth with a purpose or destiny? If so, how will you find out what that purpose is? Does having a destiny mean that you have no free will?

These are tough questions, and you won't find definitive answers to them on the Internet or in an encyclopedia. Maybe you have never really thought about things like this before. But, if you have, you are not the only one. These thoughts are not really weird, they are philosophical, and that is what this book is about.

This is the second volume of *Philosophy for Teens*. The first volume explores issues in values, aesthetics, and political philosophy, but it is not a prerequisite for this book, which stands alone (although we do hope you will also read the first volume). In this book, we explore philosophical issues in metaphysics and epistemology.

Metaphysics and *epistemology* are obnoxious words, but the ideas are really quite simple. The "physics" part just stands for science, and the "meta" means beyond. So, metaphysics just means the study of what lies beyond science. For example, no scientist can ever really prove whether or not a soul, or God, exists, but these are still meaningful questions, and when we discuss such things we are doing metaphysics.

Epistemology literally means the "science of knowledge," and when we are studying epistemology we are investigating what we know and how we know it. Some philosophers have argued that we don't know anything for sure. Others argue that we are limited to scientific knowledge. And, still others think that we can even have metaphysical knowledge. We will be looking at representatives of all of these positions.

We will also look at the issues of whether computers can think, whether we have free will, whether we are born with any innate knowledge, whether we can believe things that we cannot prove, and, of course, whether there is a "meaning of life."

These sorts of questions are difficult, but also fun and profitable. They are fun because most of us have opinions on these sorts of issues, which are revised and refined by philosophical argument. Having a philosophical argument is not a bad thing. Rather, it is a tool for helping us improve our own opinions. And, that is why considering these questions also is profitable. Think about how many opinions are "out there." Now, think about the odds that you have the very best opinion. Pretty slim, right? So by subjecting your opinion, and those of your fellow philosophers, to real critical scrutiny, you improve the chances of getting it right. There are always more discussions and opinions out there to help you revise and refine your own.

It is fun to experiment with new ideas, even though it may feel strange at first. We begin each chapter of this book with an exercise to help you get the hang of it. The exercise involves reading a dialogue between two fictional high school students and answering some questions about the dialogue. We encourage you to read the dialogues aloud with someone else, each of you adopting the role of one of the characters. Try to put yourself in your character's mind frame and see what it might be like to actually hold the view he or she advocates. You may decide to agree, or you may decide to disagree. Either way, if you have entertained the view as your own it will be easier for you to give reasons for your decision. At the end of each chapter, we challenge you to write a dialogue of your own on one of the themes we have discussed.

In the middle of each chapter you will find another type of exercise known as a "thought experiment." A thought experiment is an imaginary scenario designed to test the truth of a controversial claim. For example, suppose someone claims that religious belief is necessary to give life meaning. We could test this claim by trying to imagine lives or societies that function without religion. If we can imagine this, then the original claim is false. If we cannot imagine it, then the claim stands as a reasonable possibility. At the end of each chapter, we challenge you to construct a thought experiment to test one of the central claims made in the chapter.

Keep in mind that any book referred to in the text will be listed at the end of the chapter in the References section. You will also find a list of books and articles related to each chapter in the section marked "Further Reading." These lists will enable you to pursue issues that interest you on your own. The reading comprehension and discussion questions at the end of each chapter are designed to enhance your understanding of the concepts presented in the chapter, while the activities and exercises are designed to help you apply these concepts to your daily life. Finally, there is a glossary at the end of the book to help you keep track of new philosophical terms.

Philosophy wakes your up and makes you think. Once you get used to it, you won't know how you ever lived without it.

PART 1

The Self

Copy after Ingres's 1805 Self-Portrait, 1850–1860, Jean Auguste Dominique Ingres

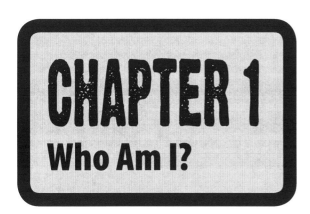

CHAPTER 1
Who Am I?

The Diary

It is around 10 p.m. Mollie is phoning her friend Andreas. Andreas is in his bedroom writing in a thick notebook when he hears the phone ring and answers it.

ANDREAS: Hello?

MOLLIE: *<Brightly>* Hey Andreas. It's Mollie. Am I calling too late?

ANDREAS: *<Andreas is still finishing a sentence he is writing in his notebook.>* Nah. I'm wide awake.

MOLLIE: *<Sensing his distraction, scowling a little>* Whatcha doin?

ANDREAS: *<Still writing>* Nothin' much. *<Suddenly embarrassed, he puts down his pen and closes the notebook.>* Actually, I was writing in my journal.

MOLLIE: *<Surprised>* You mean—like a diary?

ANDREAS: Yeah. *<He shoves the notebook under some clothing in a dresser drawer.>* I've been writing in it almost every night since my parents got divorced last year.

MOLLIE: Wow! Do you record everything you do?

ANDREAS: No. It's more like what I'm thinkin' about.

MOLLIE: Oh. *<She continues in a gentle voice.>* Like how you're mad at your mom for taking off with that other guy?

ANDREAS: Yeah, sometimes I write about how I feel. Sometimes I plan out my future. *<He takes the notebook back out of the drawer and starts flipping through it.>* Last week I recorded this really wild dream I had and tried to analyze it. *<Brightening>* It's kinda cool flipping back through the notebooks. I get a sense of who I am.

MOLLIE: Hmmm . . .

ANDREAS: *<Suddenly embarrassed again>* What's that supposed to mean?

MOLLIE: I dunno. I had a teacher once who made us keep a journal for a few weeks. We were supposed to be reflecting on "who we really are" or something. We always just made stuff up. I remember once I wrote that I thought I was the ghost of a boy in a girl's body! *<She laughs.>* That was a good one. *<Still laughing>* The teacher ate it up!

ANDREAS: It's not funny. Maybe some people really do feel like that. . . .

MOLLIE: Look, Andreas, don't get me wrong! I think it's cool you write in a journal. But, to me it's just like writing stories. You can make up whatever you want to be because there is no "secret you" inside to figure out. You just are who you are.

Questions

- What is the point of writing in a journal, according to Andreas?
- What is the point of writing in a journal, according to Mollie?
- With whom do you agree more, and why?
- Have you ever kept a journal? If so, what kinds of things did you write about? If not, would you ever consider keeping a journal? Why or why not?

•   Suppose you were writing a journal right now. What would you say? Do you think that there is a secret "you" that writing in a journal will help you discover?

Who Am I?

René Descartes
(1596–1650)

Do you ever talk to yourself? You probably do. Maybe not out loud. But, what about inside your head? For example, do you ever yell at yourself when you do something stupid? ("Idiot! I can't believe you did that again!") Or, do you congratulate yourself when you do something good? ("Oh yeah! You rock!") Many people say they hear a "little voice" inside their heads telling them what to do and what not to do. There's no question that we all talk to ourselves sometimes. The question is, when you talk to yourself, who are you talking to?

Some people think every human being has a soul. They think that your soul is the real you, and it's who you talk to when you talk to yourself. Because the soul is a nonphysical substance, it lives inside you and moves your body like a ghost in a machine. When you die, your soul can live on as a spirit without your body. This belief is an important part of many religions. Because the soul is completely invisible, however, belief in it is controversial. There is no proof that it exists.

The French philosopher René Descartes (1596–1650) believed in the existence of the soul. In his view, the soul is nothing but the mind in which all of our thoughts take place. Because the thoughts in your mind are what make you who you are, a record of your thoughts is a record of the real you.

Descartes kept a journal and published it under the title *Meditations on First Philosophy*. In it he argued that we know a lot more about our own minds than we know about anything else in the physical world. We may *think* we know a lot about the things we see and hear around us. But, our eyes and ears are often mistaken. Furthermore, when we dream, we seem to see and hear all sorts of things that aren't really real. Descartes presented a thought experiment like the one below to show that we shouldn't always trust our experience of the physical world.

Descartes dreamed about writing in his journal as often as he actually wrote in his journal. On the one hand, it bothered him that he couldn't tell for sure at any given moment whether he was awake or asleep. On the other hand, he noticed that, when it came to recording his thoughts, it didn't really matter. Those thoughts were still his thoughts whether he was awake or asleep. Even though he might be wrong about everything going on outside himself, he could not be wrong about what was going on inside.

Thought Experiment: Dreaming the Dream

Suppose that when you go to bed tonight you dream you are reading this book, just as you are now. The dream is very realistic, including all the thoughts you are thinking and writing down as you work through the chapter. Then, the dream suddenly changes, and you dream that you are waking up. In the dream you realize that you were only dreaming about reading this book. As the dream continues, you sit down to read this book and remember what you thought and wrote during the dream's dream. You feel exactly the same as you did in the dream's dream. Before long, it is morning. You wake up—for real this time—and remember dreaming that you were dreaming. The dream you had about having a dream about this book was so realistic that you can hardly believe you were only dreaming. When you sit down to read this book again, you feel exactly as you did in the dream and in the dream's dream.

Notice that as you read this book right now, you may in fact be dreaming. You may wake up in a little while and realize you weren't really reading this book, but only dreaming you were reading it. You probably feel sure you are awake, but people often feel that way during their dreams. Is there any way to determine whether you are dreaming or not?

Descartes wrote:

> But what then am I? A thinking thing. And what is that? Something that doubts, understands, affirms, denies, wills, refuses—and also imagines and senses. . . . Even if I am always dreaming . . . isn't it just as true that I do all these things as that I exist? Are any of these things distinct from my thought? Can any be said to be separate from me? It's so obvious that it is me who doubts, understands, and wills that I don't see how I could make it more evident. (From *Meditations on First Philosophy* 1641/1996, [http://wright.edu/cola/Descartes])

Descartes argued that he is a "thinking thing" because, even if his thoughts are wrong, he is still thinking them. He concluded that the physical world is not nearly as important as his mind, where his thinking takes place. This view is called *dualism* because it holds that a human being is two things: a mind and a body. According to this view, our minds are temporarily attached to our bodies during life on earth.

The main problem with dualism is that it is not clear how the soul could be attached to the body. Consider how things are normally attached to each other: with glue, tape, nails, magnets, Velcro, or the like. You could certainly attach one body to another body in any of these ways. But, none of these ways will work on a soul because a soul is not a physical object. This means it doesn't have any surface: If you tried to grab it, your hand would go right through. The problem of how the mind is connected to our heads and our hearts is called the mind-body problem. Descartes left this problem for other philosophers to solve. Do you have any ideas?

Many philosophers have given up on trying to solve this problem, concluding that there is no such thing as the soul. This view is called *materialism*, because it holds that physical matter is the only thing that exists; all our thoughts can be explained in purely physical terms. According to materialism, the belief that a spirit lives in and moves our bodies is an outdated superstition that should be rejected like other outdated superstitions. For example, people living in the Middle Ages had no explanation for why people became sick. As a result, many believed that sickness was the work of invisible demons. Today we know that those "invisible demons" are actually just viruses. Likewise, perhaps Descartes' "thinking thing" is actually just the brain. All of our thoughts, feelings, and desires are activated by neural impulses that we don't completely understand yet. The more we learn about the brain, the less we will need to believe in the soul.

Daniel Dennett (1942–) is an American philosopher who embraces materialism. He advances a theory to explain why it feels as though we have a soul even though we really don't. Because human beings are members of the animal kingdom, we can learn about ourselves by studying other animals. The one thing all animals have in common is the survival instinct. Each species has its own special way to survive. For example, spiders spin intricate webs in order to trap insects for food. Beavers build strong dams for protection against predators. Spiders and beavers do these things automatically, without even thinking about it. What makes our species, Homo sapiens, different from the rest is that

Daniel Dennett
(1942–)

we have language. Language is the special behavior we use to survive. Dennett writes:

> But the strangest and most wonderful constructions in the whole animal world are the amazing, intricate constructions made by the primate, Homo sapiens. Each normal individual of this species makes a *self*. Out of its brain it spins a web of words and deeds, and, like the other creatures, it doesn't have to know what it's doing; it just does it. . . . Our fundamental tactic of self-protection, self-control, and self-definition is not spinning webs or building dams, but telling stories, and more particularly concocting and controlling the story we tell others—and ourselves—about who we are. (From *Consciousness Explained* by Daniel Dennett, 1991, pp. 416–418)

So, according to Dennett, the soul is just an idea—the self-image that comes from the language we use to refer to one another and ourselves.

Because animals can't talk about themselves, they have no self-image. A spider can't say "I'm hungry." A beaver can't say "Help me!" Human beings, in contrast, need to talk about themselves in order to survive. If we couldn't say "I'm hungry" or "help me" we wouldn't get the food or the protection we needed. But, because language is so powerful, our use of it goes beyond basic survival. We use it to achieve emotional, intellectual, and social success. In talking about ourselves we slowly build a self-image so elaborate that we believe in it as though it had a separate existence that could survive the death of our bodies.

Fallacy Files

Ad Populum

Do you believe in ghosts? According to a recent Gallup Poll, 33% of Americans say they do. Is this information relevant when deciding for oneself whether or not to believe in them? Philosophers don't think so. Appealing to popularity is a fallacious form of reasoning called *ad populum*. Why should the popularity of a belief be relevant to whether it is true or false? After all, popular people are often no better than unpopular people and popular foods are often a lot worse than unpopular ones! In the ancient world it was very popular to believe the earth is flat. The astronomer Ptolemy (A. D. c100–c178) disagreed and he turned out to be right!

Doing philosophy provides an opportunity to reflect on who we really are. For those who agree with Descartes, this means getting in touch with our souls. For those who agree with Dennett, it means constructing a successful self-image. Regardless of which author you agree with, reflecting on who you really are is a useful and interesting thing to do.

Reading Comprehension Questions

1. What is dualism? Which philosopher holds this view?
2. What is materialism? Which philosopher holds this view?
3. Why does it not matter whether we are awake or dreaming, according to Descartes?
4. Where does the idea of the soul or self come from, according to Dennett?
5. What is the thought experiment about dreaming designed to show? Explain.

Discussion Questions

1. Review the dialogue at the beginning of this chapter. Would Andreas agree more with Descartes or Dennett? What about Mollie? Give evidence.
2. Describe an experience you have had that is difficult to explain in purely physical terms. How might you argue that it can be explained? How might you argue that it cannot?
3. Do you think it is possible that you are dreaming right now? How would you prove that you aren't?
4. Do you hear a little voice inside your head telling you what to do and what not to do? What do you think it is?

Essay Question

Do you believe you have a soul that can survive the death of your body? Discuss both sides of this debate, making reference to Descartes and Dennett. Then, resolve the debate from your own point of view, presenting an argument in standard form for your conclusion. (For an explanation of standard form, please see Appendix B at the back of this book.)

Exercises

1. Write a dialogue between Olivia and Julio. Olivia argues that ghosts exist. Julio argues that they don't.
2. Construct a thought experiment to test the claim that non-human animals have no self-image.

Activities

1. Watch the movie *Ghost*, directed by Jerry Zucker (1990). Do you think it shows how the soul could be attached to the body?
2. Write a poem that captures your self-image.
3. Write in a journal every day for one month.
4. Interview some people at your school to find out whether they believe in ghosts and why.
5. Make a list of old-fashioned superstitions that have been replaced by modern scientific explanations.

References

Dennett, D. C. (1991). *Consciousness explained*. Boston, MA: Little, Brown, and Company.

Descartes, R. (1996). *Meditations on first philosophy* (D. B. Manley & C. S. Taylor, Trans.). Retrieved April 26, 2007, from http://wright.edu/cola/descartes. (Original work published 1641)

Further Reading

Dennett, D. C. (2006, January 24). The nonbeliever. *The New York Times Magazine*, p. 21.

Gottfried, G. M. (2003). "I just talk with my heart": The mind–body problem, linguistic input, and the acquisition of folk psychological beliefs. *Cognitive Development, 18*, 79–91.

Hansen, C. M. (2000). Between a rock and a hard place: Mental causation and the mind-body problem. *Inquiry, 43*, 451–492.

Kirk, R. (1993). "The Best Set of Tools?" Dennett's metaphors and the mind-body problem. *Philosophical Quarterly, 43*, 335–344.

Peck, S. L. (2003). Randomness, contingency, and faith: Is there a science of subjectivity? *Zygon: Journal of Religion & Science, 38*, 5–24.

Ryle, G. (1949). *Descartes' myth and the concept of mind*. London: Hutchinson.

Secada, J. (2003). Learning to understand Descartes. *Philosophical Quarterly, 53*, 437–446.

Swinburne, R. (2003). Body and soul. *Think, 5*, 28–39.

Thomasson, M. (1996). Practical solipsism, or how to live in a world of your own. *Philosophy Now, 16*, 11–25.

Updike, J. (2004). Mind body problems. *The New Yorker, 79*(44), 90–95.

CHAPTER 2
Am I the Same Person I Used to Be?

The Reunion

Freddy and Shanique grew up in the same neighborhood. After high school they went off to different colleges. They are now home for Christmas break, meeting at a diner where they used to hang out.

FREDDY: *<Walking in and spotting Shanique by the window.>* Hey girl—you look great!

SHANIQUE: *<Giving him a big hug.>* So do you. You must have grown 4 inches.

FREDDY: Yeah, but I'm the same old me! *<They sit down.>*

SHANIQUE: I'm the same old me too. But, have you seen Monica yet? She is so different.

FREDDY: Yeah, I ran into her last night. *<Grinning.>* She used to be so quiet and shy. Now she wants to take on the world.

SHANIQUE: I know. We went shopping together last week. She talked a blue streak about life in Europe and bought some pretty outrageous clothes.

FREDDY: Yeah, she's stylin' now. *<Sheepishly>* I actually asked her out for Friday.

SHANIQUE: *<Gaping>* You did? I don't even really like her any more.

FREDDY: Oh, come off it. You two have been friends forever.

SHANIQUE: I'm telling you—she's a different person.

FREDDY: Give me a break. Someone can't become a different person.

SHANIQUE: Sure she can. A person is just a set of qualities. If you start with one set and exchange all the qualities in it for new qualities, then you have a new set.

FREDDY: A person isn't just a set of qualities. A person has a soul that contains all their qualities. Even when the qualities change, the soul stays the same. <*He raises his eyebrows and looks pointedly at her.*> I think you're just jealous.

SHANIQUE: <*Indignant*> Yeah, right! I'm just trying to save you from this imposter.

FREDDY: <*Laughing*> Maybe the new Monica is actually an evil twin.

SHANIQUE: <*Laughing*> Or, a robot . . .

FREDDY: Or, maybe she just had a brain transplant. What do I care? I like her better now.

SHANIQUE: <*Suddenly somber and serious*> But, what about me? I miss the old Monica. Can you stay friends with someone who's changed so much?

FREDDY: Sure, people change all the time. You don't usually notice because it happens little by little. For Monica, it happened fast while we were out of touch.

SHANIQUE: I don't think we can save our old friendship, but I guess I'm willing to try to make a new one. At any rate, somebody's got to warn her about you!

Questions

- Why does Shanique think one person can become a different person?
- Why does Freddy think this is impossible?

- With whom do you agree more, and why?
- Describe a time when someone you know was acting like a different person.
- Do you think people have souls that always stay the same? Why or why not?
- Do you think it is possible for someone to have a brain transplant? Explain.

Am I the Same Person I Used to Be?

Try to remember what it was like to be you 10 years ago. Are you the same person today? You certainly don't look the same. You also know a lot more than you did then and you act differently. Furthermore, over time new cells have replaced most of the cells that were in your body 10 years ago. Of course, you probably have the same name. But, your name doesn't define you, because you can change your name and still be you. Pick a new name right now and pretend that you are going to move to a new city. When you meet new people there, you will tell them your new name. Suppose you also dye your hair and buy new clothes. After 10 years away you are unrecognizable to anyone in your old town, even your own family members. Would you still be *you*?

There are two different kinds of change: continuity and succession. In continuity, one thing remains throughout the change despite being different at the end. For example, a banana undergoes a change of continuity when it ripens from green to yellow to brown. In succession, one thing changes into another thing. For example, a caterpillar turns into a butterfly in a change of succession.

Do human beings change in the first way or in the second way? On the one hand, you could compare your life to the ripening of a banana: You are one person taking on different qualities with age. On the other hand, if you think about it, the difference between a baby and an elderly person is extreme, much like the difference between a caterpillar and a butterfly. Are you one continuous thing throughout your life or are you a succession of things? This is known as the problem of personal identity, and it has vexed philosophers for centuries. The following thought experiment illustrates why it is so hard to tell whether one thing remains throughout a change or turns into something else.

John Locke
(1632–1704)

John Locke (1632–1704) was an English philosopher who supported the *continuity theory*—that each person is one continuous thing throughout life. For Locke, it doesn't matter if our bodies change drastically during that time. In fact, one and the same person could come to inhabit a totally different body. This is exactly what happens to human beings who go to heaven, according to Locke. Upon death, your physical body decomposes, while you live on in a new spiritual body in heaven. This is a radical change: Your new heavenly body will have none of the same matter or form as your earthly body. And yet, you will still be you. How is this possible?

Locke had an answer: memory. When you go to heaven, you will be able to remember living your life on Earth. You will not remember living anyone else's life, and no one else will be able to remember living your life. Your memories are completely unique and they have shaped your personality. You are who you are based on the experiences you have had. No one can ever take those away from you or know what they were like from the inside.

Although memory helps to explain how each person stays him- or herself when he or she moves from Earth to the afterlife, it also helps to explain how each person stays him- or herself throughout life on Earth. The change from infancy to elderly years is extreme. As time goes by you look and feel like a completely different person. But, you're not really, according to Locke, because your memories connect you to your past. You remember that it was *you* that fell down the stairs at age 4. You can still remember the pain even if there are no physical scars. And, 10 years from now, you will remember that it was *you* who read this book 10 years ago. Even if you had an identical twin, or if you were to be cloned, memory is what would keep you distinct from the twin or the clone.

Of course, you can't remember your entire life. There may be vast stretches of time that you can't picture at all. But for Locke, this doesn't matter. Those memories are still there, buried deep in your mind. (This is evident in that people often recall forgotten pieces of the past when they have a reminder, such as a photograph, and hypnosis is a well-known method for revisiting forgotten experiences.) Locke wrote:

> For as far as any intelligent being *can* repeat the idea of any past action with the same consciousness it had of it at first, and with the same consciousness it has of any present action; so far it is the same personal self. For it is by the con-

Thought Experiment: The Ship of Theseus

Imagine that your friend Theseus buys a little wooden ship. He names it "The Marlin" and carefully follows a preventative maintenance program. Every month, he takes one old plank off, replacing it with a new plank. Most of us would say that it is the same ship; after all, you don't claim to have a new car when you get a new tire. This maintenance goes on for years. All the while, you secretly collect the old planks. When Theseus finally replaces the last original plank, you reconstruct all of the old planks, including the one that has "The Marlin" painted on it, into a ship. So now, the question arises: Who owns the Marlin? On the one hand, Theseus bought the Marlin, named it, and took care of it for many years. He never sold it or gave it to you. On the other hand, your ship has the same shape as Theseus's ship and is made of the Marlin's original planks. Which ship is the Marlin? Both? Neither? How does this story relate to the life of a human being?

One final twist: Would it make any difference to your answers if the ship in question was of historical significance, one of Columbus' ships, for example? Imagine that all of the wood of the original ship on display in the museum has been replaced over the years. We still call it Columbus' ship. But now, suppose that the curator has taken all of the original wood and reassembled it in his backyard. Which one has historic value?

sciousness it has of its present thoughts and actions, that it is self to itself now, and so will be the same self, as far as the same consciousness can extend to actions past or to come, and would be by distance of time, or change of substance, no more two persons, than a man be two men by wearing other clothes to-day than he did yesterday, with a long or a short sleep between: the same consciousness uniting those distant actions into the same person, whatever substances contributed to their production. (From *An Essay Concerning Human Understanding,* by John Locke, 1690, [http://ethnicity.rutgers.edu/~jlynch/Texts/locke227.html])

Changing bodily form is a superficial difference just like changing clothes, according to Locke.

Although Locke's view seems like common sense, it does have some strange implications. Imagine the case of a prince who wakes up one morning to find himself in the body of a pauper. The prince still remembers being crowned and ruling his kingdom. So, according to the continuity theory, the prince is still the prince, and he should be allowed to continue his rule, even though he no

Derek Parfit
(1942–)

longer looks the part. Locke is happy to admit this implication, but he fails to consider further problems pointed out by the English philosopher Derek Parfit (1942–).

Parfit rejects Locke's continuity theory in favor of the *succession theory*—that each person is a succession of beings throughout life. A prince who woke up in a little girl's body would be a different person, according to Parfit, and he would not be able to go on ruling in a country that only allowed male rulers. Think about it: He may remember some things about ruling in the past, but memories are notoriously unreliable. Furthermore, the prince now has the brain, the voice, the desires, and the stature of a little girl. He wouldn't be allowed to do his job, and some would argue that he wouldn't be able to do his job.

The case of the prince and the little girl provides a good illustration for Parfit's view of the change that each person actually experiences throughout life. When you are 20, you can remember some of the things you did when you were 4, but you can't do them anymore. (If you doubt this, try eating lots of cheap candy and watching kiddie cartoons over and over again like you used to!) Likewise, when you're 50, you may remember experiences you had when you were 20, but you can't relive them. Nor would you want to! (Think about competing on the school track team at age 50.) Have you ever noticed how so many of the things you used to do for fun don't even sound appealing any more? This shows that you are not the same person you used to be.

Parfit uses science fiction to update the case of the prince and the little girl. Suppose that, in the future, scientists perfect teletransportation, a mode of travel portrayed in many science fiction movies, such as *Star Trek*. Here is how it works: You enter a booth where a machine scans the type and position of every atom in your body, then painlessly destroys the body. This information is immediately sent to your destination where another machine reconstructs your body from the plan. It doesn't matter that the machine is using different atoms, because the ones in your body right now are being replaced all of the time anyway. So, you step into the transporter and it recreates you in the machine at your destination. But—oops!—a malfunction occurs and the teletransporter recreates you at two different destinations. Now, there are two of you, with identical bodies and all the same memories. This shows that memory does not guarantee uniqueness and therefore cannot be the answer to the problem of personal identity as Locke thought. Without this answer, continuity theory falls apart.

Parfit is happy to concede instead that each person is a succession of beings throughout life. In his view, you are related to your past selves in much the same way that you are related to your family members: You care about them, and take responsibility for them, but only up to a point, because ultimately they are not you. Just as your past selves are not you, your future selves are not you either. So, your future self might make it to heaven, but it won't be *you*. Your existence is no further fact beyond the experiences you are having right now. Parfit writes:

> The truth is very different from what we are inclined to believe. . . . Is the truth depressing? Some may find it so. But I find it liberating and consoling. When I believed that my existence was such a further fact, I seemed imprisoned in myself. My life seemed like a glass tunnel, through which I was moving faster every year, and at the end of which there was darkness. When I changed my view, the walls of my glass tunnel disappeared. I now live in the open air. There is still a difference between my life and the lives of other people. But the difference is less. Other people are closer. I am less concerned about the rest of my own life, and more concerned about the lives of others. (From *Reasons and Persons* by Derek Parfit, 1984, p. 281)

Parfit indicates that identifying with the past and the future makes it hard to appreciate the present. Rather than focusing your attention vertically on the timeline running between the past and the future, you should focus your attention horizontally, on everything else happening around you right now. You will then be able appreciate how the experiences of others intersect with your experiences.

Is Parfit correct to suppose that he is a succession of beings? One way to focus this question is to consider our attitude toward criminals. Does it make sense to hold a 50-year-old man responsible for a crime he committed when he was 20? Suppose that, while in prison, he earns a college degree and comes to devote most of his free time to a charity program. Some would say that he is a new man now. On the other hand, it is very difficult for human beings not to identify with their past selves. A 50-year-old may still feel guilty for a crime he committed when he was 20. Furthermore, suppose this same man got married at age 20 and never divorced. Because, in Parfit's view, it was not he, but his past self who said the vows, do you think that these vows are still binding? Parfit's succession theory raises all kinds of interesting questions about whether anything really lasts.

```
Fallacy Files
```

Loaded Definition

It is always important to be as clear as possible when you make your point. Often this will involve defining your terms. But, philosophers also try to avoid defining their terms in a way that is "loaded." A *loaded definition* is biased to favor one side of the argument over the other. For example, if you defined abortion as "the killing of an unborn person," you would be loading the definition. The reason is that it is already against the law to kill people. So, if abortion is killing a person then it has to be wrong. But, many people do not think abortion is wrong precisely because they do not think it constitutes the killing of a person. Instead, they would define abortion as the "destruction of a fetus." There may be some argument over which definition is less biased. It is usually best if you keep searching until you find one neutral definition upon which both sides can agree.

Reading Comprehension Questions

1. What is the continuity theory of personal identity? Which philosopher holds this view?
2. What is the succession theory of personal identity? Which philosopher holds this view?
3. What makes it possible for a single person to persist through radical change, according to Locke?
4. How does Parfit prove that memory does not guarantee uniqueness?
5. What is the Ship of Theseus thought experiment designed to show? Explain.

Discussion Questions

1. Review the dialogue at the beginning of this chapter. Would Shanique agree more with Locke or with Parfit? What about Freddy? Give evidence.

2. Describe an experience that made you feel like you were a different person. How might you argue that you were? How might you argue that you were not?
3. Suppose the teletransportation machine has been widely and safely used for a number of years. Would you use this method of transportation? Why or why not?
4. Suppose you were involved in an accident that destroyed most of your body below the neck. However, your brain can be saved and implanted in a body very much like the one you had. Would you still be you? If, in the same situation, the new body is mechanical, would you still be you?

Essay Question

Do you believe you are one continuous thing throughout your lifetime or that you are a succession of things? Discuss both sides of this debate, making reference to Locke and Parfit. Then, resolve the debate from your own point of view, presenting an argument in standard form for your conclusion.

Exercises

1. Write a dialogue between a prince and a cobbler who have swapped memories and meet in the marketplace.
2. Construct a thought experiment to test the claim that memories are a reliable connection to the past.

Activities

1. Watch the movie *All of Me*, directed by Carl Reiner (1984). What can this tell us about the results of memory swaps between the sexes?
2. Research split personality disorders. What, if anything, do these disorders tell us about personal identity?

3. Watch the movie *The Fly*, directed by David Cronenberg (1986). What does this film suggest about the importance of the physical body to personal identity?
4. Read Mary Wollstonecraft Shelley's *Frankenstein*. Do you think that what starts out as the "monster" becomes a person? If so, what makes him a person?
5. Watch the movie, *Freaky Friday*, directed by Mark Waters (2003). What do you think it is saying about personal identity?

References

Locke, J. (n.d.). *An essay concerning human understanding* (Book II, Chapter 9ff). Retrieved April 30, 2007, from http://ethnicity.rutgers.edu/~jlynch/Texts/locke227.html (Original work published in 1690)

Parfit, D. (1984). *Reasons and persons*. Oxford, England: Clarendon Press.

Further Reading

Kind, A. (2004). The metaphysics of personal identity and our special concern for the future. *Metaphilosophy, 35,* 536–553.

Noonan, H. (Ed.). (1993). *Personal identity*. Brookfield, VT: Dartmouth Publishing.

Rachels, S., & Alter, T. (2005). Nothing matters in survival. *Journal of Ethics, 9,* 311–330.

Rivas, T. (2005). Rebirth and personal identity: Is reincarnation an intrinsically impersonal concept?" *Journal of Religion & Psychical Research, 28,* 226–233.

Shoemaker, S. (1975). Personal identity and memory. In J. Perry (Ed.), *Personal identity* (pp. 119–134). Los Angeles: University of California Press.

Tittle, P. (2005). *What if . . . Collected Thought Experiments in philosophy*. New York, NY: Pearson Longman.

Webster, R. S. (2005). Personal identity: Moving beyond essence. *International Journal of Children's Spirituality, 10,* 5–16.

Williams, B. (1957). Personal identity and individuation. *Proceedings of the Aristotelian Society, 57,* 229–252.

CHAPTER 3
Am I Free?

The Movie

Mike and Sierra are going to the movies on their first date. In the car on the way to the theater, they realize they have a choice between two different movies playing at the same time: an action thriller and a romantic comedy. Mike prefers the first and Sierra prefers the second.

MIKE: Look at us—being the typical guy and girl! *<He laughs, shaking his head.>*

SIERRA: *<Annoyed, glaring at him a little>* What do you mean?

MIKE: Guys know how to appreciate a good fight, you know? But, girls always just go for the lovey-dovey stuff. *<He makes kissing noises.>* "Ohhhhhhh Harry!" *<more noises>* "Kiss me, kiss me, kiss me!"

SIERRA: Shut up, Mike! *<She laughs a little, in spite of herself.>* Maybe romantic comedies are more popular with girls, but that has nothing to do with my choice. *<Serious now>* I never go to action movies because I'm against violence.

MIKE: Oh, come on. Now you're just tryin' to make me feel bad. Think you can trick me into going to your movie, huh? *<He grins at her.>*

SIERRA: *<She smirks.>* I'm just saying that everybody's free to choose. And, the choices you make determine what kind of person you become.

MIKE: <*Rolling his eyes*> It isn't a choice for guys to like violence! We're built for it. <*He sees her raise her eyebrows.*> I'm serious! Ever since caveman days, that's how men have survived—by fighting. So, it's in my nature. Besides that, it's reinforced as we grow up. No little boy wants to be called a sissy on the playground.

SIERRA: Mike, that's the lamest excuse I've ever heard. <*She pauses, thinking.*> You're basically saying you have no choice in life—that your nature and your upbringing determine who you are.

MIKE: <*Nodding his head*> Well, it's true, isn't it? You say we're free to choose. If we're so free then how come everything we do is so predictable? Did you know insurance companies can predict how many suicides there will be in a given area in a given year? They predict all kinds of other stuff, too. Some day, with better computers, we'll be able to predict everything.

SIERRA: Not me, pal. It may be true that most people just go with the flow. They don't exercise their freedom to choose. But, I do. You better believe it! I do all kinds of unpredictable things, <*she taps her finger to her lip*> . . . like going out with you.

MIKE: A good-looking guy like me? I'm irresistible. Where's the choice in that?

Questions

- Why does Sierra think humans are free to choose?
- Why doesn't Mike think so?
- With whom do you agree more, and why?
- Have you ever made a free choice? If so, what was it, how do you know it was free, and how would you prove it? If not, why do you think so many people think they have made free choices?
- Have you ever predicted exactly what someone was about to do? Explain how this might be possible.

Am I Free?

Have you ever felt like the things you do are not really up to you? There are so many influences on us that affect the choices we make. These influences come from two main sources.

First, there's your biological makeup. Consider Janey. She loves sports and finds art really boring. So, she chose to spend her free time last summer playing on a softball team rather than taking a watercolor class. She inherited an athletic build from her parents, making her a good softball player. If she had been built with artistic talent instead, she probably would have made the opposite choice for how to spend her free time. She's becoming an athlete rather than an artist, and her biological makeup is playing a big role in this.

Then, there's your environment. Carlos is a good example. At his old school he was hanging out with a tough gang. He smoked and drank a lot and was on the verge of failing and being expelled from school. Then, his family moved to a small town where there were no gangs. He hated it at first, but soon he started dating a girl who is planning to go to college. Now, Carlos is getting better grades and staying out of trouble. Clearly his environment influenced his change.

Janey and Carlos both feel like they're making free choices to do what they want to do. But, how free are our choices if they're determined by our biological makeup and/or our environment? One or the other or both seem to influence everything we do, even if we aren't aware of it. In fact, it seems as though humans are just like computers. Our biology is our hardware and what we absorb from our environment becomes our input. Although computers can do amazing things, they aren't free. Are we? The following thought experiment shows how human beings may be different from computers.

C. A. Campbell (1897–1974) was a Scottish philosopher who argued that human beings do make free choices. Granting that our biological makeup and our environment determine much of what we do, he maintains that whenever we make a moral choice, we act freely. An example of a moral choice would be when you treat people nicely even when you're in a bad mood. Can you think of other examples?

Why would moral choices be free? Campbell argued that our biology and our environment determine our desires. Recall that Janey's desire to play softball came from her athletic build and

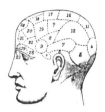

Thought Experiment: Buridan's Tie

Imagine you're a computer hacker and you devise an ingenious program that can instantly shut down any computer. It's based on a simple idea: The program instructs the computer to do opposite things. In particular, typing the letter "p" triggers "print" and "don't print" at the same time. Receiving opposite instructions causes the computer to freeze because it can't do both at the same time, and it has no way to break the tie between the two commands. Now, suppose you encode a similar program on a chip and implant it in your friend Buridan's brain. In this case, saying "go" to Buridan triggers conflicting impulses in him: He wants to jump up and squat down at the same time. But, of course he can't do both. Do you think he would freeze and shut down, like the computer or do you think he could override the commands in order to break the tie? A computer would have to be programmed how to override the dual commands. Would a human? Some people think of free choice as breaking a tie between two equal possibilities.

Carlos's desire to get good grades came from being at a new school. When we just do whatever our desires tell us to do, we're letting our biological makeup and our environment determine us. But, a moral choice is a choice that sometimes goes against your strongest desire. For example, everybody has a bad day now and then that puts him or her in a bad mood. When you're in a bad mood, the last thing you want to do is treat people nicely. Choosing to be nice in spite of your mood means resisting your desire. It shows that there is something in you beyond your biological and environmental programming that makes you free. Campbell wrote:

> When we decide to exert moral effort to resist a temptation, we feel quite certain that we could withhold the effort; just as, if we decide to withhold the effort and yield to our

desires, we feel quite certain that we could exert it—otherwise we should not blame ourselves afterwards for having succumbed. . . . the very essence of the moral decision as it is experienced is that it is a decision whether or not to combat our strongest desire. (From *On Selfhood and Godhood*, by C. A. Campbell, 1957, p. 164)

Campbell's view is called *libertarianism*, because it asserts that human beings are at liberty to make free choices.

Percy Brand Blanshard (1892–1987) was an American philosopher who disagreed with Campbell. In his view, all of our actions are determined by a combination of our biological makeup and our environment. When you make a moral choice, you may feel as though you're resisting your strongest desire. But really, you're just obeying a different kind of desire, namely, a moral one. As we grow up, we absorb moral desires from various influences in our environment: church, teachers, parents, books, etc. These moral desires sometimes conflict with desires stemming from our biological makeup or other environmental influences. When they do, we may feel paralyzed at first, not sure what to do, like a computer programmed with conflicting instructions. But, as we think more about the situation, one or another of the conflicting desires will emerge as the strongest and break the tie.

Percy Brand Blanshard
(1892–1987)

According to Blanshard's beliefs, human beings always have to obey their strongest desire. We just have to hope that our strongest desires are good ones. Blanshard wrote:

Many an artist and musician have left it on record that their best work was done when the piece they were creating took on a life of its own and seemed to complete itself. That is, the artist is saying that there was only one possible way for the piece to be completed. It determined them, but they were free, because to be determined by this whole was at once the secret of their craft and the end of their desire. This is the condition of the moral man also. He has caught a vision . . . a vision of the good. This good necessitates certain things, not as means to ends merely, for that is not usually a necessary link, but as integral parts of itself. (From "The Case for Determinism," by Percy Brand Blanshard, 1958, p. 29)

Blanshard's view is called *determinism*, because it holds that everything we do is determined by desires stemming from our biological makeup or our environment.

According to Blanshard, human beings are never able to do anything other than what they in fact do. We feel as though we can, but this is just an illusion caused by the fact that we aren't aware of all of the influences determining us. Blanchard was convinced that, if we could accurately record all the influences and measure exactly how much they affect us, we would be able to predict everything we do. Note that you can often predict what a friend or relative will do before that person can because you have a better perspective on what influences are at work.

As we've seen, Campbell maintained that we wouldn't be able to blame people for doing wrong if they couldn't help it. But, determinists insist that we can and should. The reason is that it helps to create an environment that will influence people in the right way. Being blamed is an unpleasant experience—no one wants to be punished or yelled at. The desire to avoid blame can help counteract the desire to make an immoral choice. You'll be less likely to mistreat people when you're in a bad mood if you know you'll be punished or yelled at later. In this way, blame functions in an important way to reinforce moral desires.

Although determinists maintain a role for blame in their view, it's very different from the role blame plays in the libertarian's view. For the libertarian, when you blame someone, you're saying it's his or her fault and he or she deserves to pay for it. For the determinist, when you blame someone, you're not saying it's his or her fault, because what he or she did was caused by his or her biological makeup and environment. Nor does it make sense to make him or her pay for what these influences made him or her do. Instead, you're just trying to give him or her and others incentive never to do it again. These two different ways of thinking about blame affect the way people feel about the prison system, parenting, and many other aspects of life.

Fallacy Files

Weasel Word

Despite all of their disagreement, Campbell and Blanshard agree that human beings are free. How can this be? Each has a different definition of the word. For Campbell, being free means being able to resist your strongest desire. For Blanshard, being free means being able to act on your strongest desire without interference from someone else. These are two very different understandings of the word *free*. Philosophers call words with double meanings *weasel words*, because their definitions are tricky. Fortunately, both Campbell and Blanshard are careful to stick to their own definitions. But, someone who was less careful might slip from one meaning of the word to the other without noticing. This makes it impossible to pin down their true view. If you're using a word that can have two meanings, be sure to explain which meaning you're using and stick to it.

Reading Comprehension Questions

1. What is libertarianism? Which philosopher holds this view?
2. What is determinism? Which philosopher holds this view?
3. What is a moral choice, according to Campbell?
4. What is the purpose of blame and punishment, according to determinists?
5. What is the thought experiment about Buridan's tie designed to show? Explain.

Discussion Questions

1. Review the dialogue at the beginning of this chapter. Would Mike agree more with Campbell or Blanshard? What about Sierra? Give evidence.
2. Describe a big choice you made in the past. Looking back, does it seem like you could have done otherwise? Why or why not?
3. Does it ever make sense to blame someone for doing something when he or she couldn't help it in your view? Explain.
4. Does believing in free choice make a difference in the way a person lives his or her life? Use an example to show that it does or does not.

Essay Question

Do you believe you are free? Discuss both sides of this debate, making reference to Campbell and Blanshard. Then, resolve the debate from your own point of view, presenting an argument in standard form for your conclusion.

Exercises

1. Write a dialogue between Cesar and Cindy. Cesar argues the purpose of prison should be to make criminals suffer for their crimes. Cindy argues that it should be to give the criminals incentive to change.
2. Construct a thought experiment to test the claim that, if we could accurately record every influence and measure exactly how much they affect us, we would be able to predict everything we do.

Activities

1. Watch the movie *Terminator 3*, directed by Jonathan Mostow (2003). What do you think it shows about free choice?
2. Write a story about someone who tries to change history by going back in time and making a different choice.
3. Think of a recent moral choice you made. Make a list of all the influences that may have caused you to make that choice.
4. Present a series of choices to your best friend and see if your knowledge of him or her enables you to predict what he or she will choose.
5. Interview your parents or guardians concerning their views of free will. How does this affect their views of blame and punishment?

References

Blanshard, P. B. (1958). The case for determinism. In S. Hook (Ed.), *Determinism and freedom in the age of modern science* (pp. 19–30). New York: New York University Press.

Campbell, C. A. (1957). *On selfhood and Godhood.* New York, NY: HarperCollins.

Further Reading

Dennett, D. C. (1996). *Elbow room: The varieties of free will worth wanting.* Cambridge, MA: MIT Press.

Norwitz, M. (1991). Free will and determinism. *Philosophy Now, 1*, 15–23.

Obhi, S. S., & Haggard, P. (2004). Free will and free won't. *American Scientist, 92*, 358–366.

Pereboom, D. (1997). *Free will.* Indianapolis, IN: Hackett.

Pinker, S. (2003). Are your genes to blame? *Time, 161*(3), 98–100.

Rachels, J. (2002). Doing without free will. *Dialogue, 19*, 35–39.

Searle, J. R. (2001). Free will as a problem in neurobiology. *Philosophy, 76*, 491–515.

Spezio, M. (2004). Freedom in the body: The physical, the causal, and the possibility of choice. *Zygon, 39*, 577–591.

CHAPTER 4
How Should I Live?

The Dare

Brandy and Nicole have been shopping all morning. Their bus home is due in half an hour. They buy sodas and sit down on a bench outside the store to wait.

BRANDY: *<Sighing loudly>* Well, I'm exhausted. But, I'm really happy with the deals I found. *<She paws through her bags.>*

NICOLE: Yeah, me too. *<Pulling a necklace out of one of her bags.>* The best thing of all is this! *<She unclasps it and puts it on.>*

BRANDY: *<Looking closer at the necklace, puzzled>* I don't remember you buying that. How much was it?

NICOLE: *<Looks around slyly and then whispers>* It was free!

BRANDY: *<Blank at first and then getting the idea>* Nicole, did you steal that?

NICOLE: It's no big deal! People do it all the time. Lord knows I buy enough in these stores to deserve a bonus now and then. Everything is overpriced.

BRANDY: *<Shocked>* I can't believe you shoplift.

NICOLE: You're just scared of getting caught. I dare you to try it sometime.

BRANDY: No way. It's wrong.

NICOLE: <*Disappointed*> Well, it may be wrong for you, but not for me.

BRANDY: No, I mean stealing is *morally* wrong. It's wrong for everybody.

NICOLE: Who are you to say what's right and wrong for everybody? <*Irritated*> It takes courage to steal.

BRANDY: That's not how it works. You don't get to make up your own morality. Morality is the same for everyone.

NICOLE: Don't you see you're just buying into the system? I refuse to be just like everybody else.

BRANDY: Shoplifting doesn't make you unique. You said yourself that "people do it all the time." Why don't you strangle someone with that necklace? Now, that would be unique.

NICOLE: Nah, I'm against murder.

BRANDY: That's a relief. But, why? If you get to make up your own morality, and you're into courage, why not go all the way?

NICOLE: <*Thoughtful*> Well, maybe . . . if someone really needed killing.

BRANDY: <*Shocked again*> I never realized you were like this . . .

NICOLE: Look Brandy, everybody chooses their own morality whether they admit it or not. I respect your choice. Why can't you respect mine?

Questions

- Why does Brandy think stealing is wrong for everybody?
- Why does Nicole think it's not wrong for her?
- With whom do you agree more, and why?
- Have you ever had a conflict with a friend over values? If so, how did it make you feel? If not, how would it make you feel?
- Describe a time when someone questioned your morals. Do you think what you did was wrong or do you think the questioning showed lack of respect? Explain.

How Should I Live?

When you are little, you tend to think everyone lives just like you. You meet kids at school and assume that their homes are more or less the same as yours. As you grow up, however, you learn that there are often significant differences. For example, at Stacy's house there is no eating in the living room and no staying out past 10 p.m. on school nights. At Aaron's, in contrast, you can eat wherever you want and stay out until whenever you want, but you are never allowed to wear your shoes past the front door. Also, while Stacy's mom doesn't mind swearing, Aaron's mom will ask you to leave if she hears you swear. Every home has its own set of rules, and sometimes the differences show in public. For example, some families don't eat meat, some smoke cigarettes, and some go to church while others don't. There are so many different lifestyles!

For some people, lifestyle differences are uncomfortable or even scary. But, almost everyone goes through a stage, usually during his or her teenage years, when the idea of something different seems exciting and attractive. You realize that the set of rules you've been living under are not a necessity but a choice. You become interested in choosing a different set of rules for yourself. Known as *teenage rebellion*, this often causes a great deal of strife at home.

Those who set out to make their own rules often become moral relativists. *Moral relativism* is the view that right and wrong both depend on the person—there are no universal moral truths. Relativism is appealing because it enables you to disagree with people without having to tell them they're wrong. Suppose Ingrid decides to have an abortion and her parents get mad. Instead of fighting with them over who's right, she can simply insist that they should respect her values. Relativism seems to help preserve peace and harmony while allowing for significant differences.

Ruth Benedict (1887–1948) was an American anthropologist who advocated moral relativism. She spent a good part of her career observing different societies all around the world. Throughout her travels she was struck by how different their values were. For example, in India, someone who went into a trance was admired as a mystic; whereas, in the United States, the same person would more likely be taken to the hospital for mental illness. Just as values vary from place to place, they vary from time to time. For example, in ancient Greece, it was cool to be gay. By

Ruth Benedict
(1887–1948)

contrast, gays were arrested and killed in Nazi Germany. Benedict noticed that, despite their differences, the members of each society typically believed that they were right and that anyone who did not conform was wrong. Can you think of other examples?

Relativists argue that it is absurd to impose your own values onto others. They point out that, even within one society, there are always some deviants who refuse to conform. According to Benedict, conformity is a habit that some choose to accept and others choose to reject. She wrote:

> Mankind has always preferred to say, "It is a moral good," rather than "It is habitual". . . But historically the two phrases are synonymous. . . . The vast majority of individuals in any group are shaped to the fashion of that culture. In other words, most individuals are plastic to the molding force of the society into which they are born. In a society that values trance, as in India, they will have supernormal experience. In a society that institutionalizes homosexuality, they will be homosexual. In a society that sets the gathering of possessions as the chief human objective, they will amass property. The deviants, whatever the type of behavior the culture has institutionalized, will remain few in number. . . . (From "Anthropology and the Abnormal," by Ruth Benedict, 1934, p. 61)

A society might criticize or punish its deviant members for bad behavior, but if these same deviants had been born at another time or in another place they may have been admired and praised instead for the very same behavior. Why not just realize that values are relative and respect each person's choices?

All philosophers agree that it is good to be tolerant of different lifestyles.

Moral objectivists argue, however, that relativists have gone too far. To see whether this is the case, threaten to do something that a relativist thinks is wrong (such as hurting that person), while saying "It is right for me." Will the relativist still be a relativist in this situation? Objectivists argue that relativists have gone too far because there is an important difference between lifestyle and morality—how late you stay out is a matter of lifestyle and there is no right or wrong answer, whereas abortion is a matter of morality, and there is a right answer and a wrong answer (even if the answer is hard to find). *Moral objectivism* holds that there are universal moral truths, even though we may not always know what they are, and may not always agree about them. The following thought experiment is designed to test the relativist claim that there are no such truths.

Thought Experiment: Hansel and Gretel Stew

Suppose your new friend Darek brings you to his eccentric aunt's house for dinner. You arrive early and are invited to watch her cook the stew. In the kitchen, Darek's aunt has two small children bound and gagged in a large pot. After adding a few potatoes, carrots, and onions to the pot, she beckons Darek over to help her hoist it into a gigantic oven. As he moves to help her, you grab his arm. "Darek," you whisper, "is she putting those children in the oven?" "Yes, it seems so," Darek answers, and moves once again to help her. You grab his arm again. "Darek," you whisper, "Do you realize that those children will die in that oven?" "Yes, that seems to be the idea," Darek answers with a shrug. Once again, he moves to help his aunt. You grab his arm yet again. "Darek," you whisper, "can't you see that this is wrong?" Darek thinks about it, and then replies: "I see that the children are going in the oven, and I see that they will die, but I don't see anything wrong. I told you this dinner would be different. If you don't like it you don't have to stay."

What would you say to Darek? Would you do anything to save the children?

Judith Jarvis Thomson (1929–) is an American philosopher who rejects relativism in favor of objectivism. Thomson argues that "right" and "wrong" are adjectives that describe the world in the same way that color words do. Try to remember how you first learned your colors. Most likely someone older than you would point to something and say "This is blue" or "This is red." Before long you were able to make these identifications all by yourself. Suppose you now see a new object that you never saw before, and you correctly identify it as blue. How is this possible? Because everything that is blue has an objectively observable quality that is similar to the first blue item you observed. Whenever you see an object with

Judith Jarvis Thomson
(1929–)

this quality, you know it belongs in the same category. Imagine that your devious Uncle Frank tries to mix you up by telling you all the wrong names for colors. His trick will not work for long, and you will soon find out the truth, because everyone is in fundamental agreement about color.

The only time people disagree about colors is when it comes to "borderline cases." For example, suppose you go to school in a brick building. Because the bricks are red with a tinge of yellow, some students call the building orange while others call it red. Which is it really? It all depends on how we define these colors, and the definitions may vary. Suppose a scientist tells us that, technically, red is any color that emits wavelength "xyz." Then we can measure the wavelength of the color of the school and determine that, technically, it is red. A professional painter, however, might disagree with the scientist's definition, and call the building orange. In borderline cases, even experts disagree and there is no ultimate expert who can settle the question once and for all. Despite this, there is no reason to conclude that colors are different for everybody.

Thomson insists that the same idea applies to morality. Although there are some difficult borderline cases, there is no reason to conclude that values are different for everybody. She writes,

> The point I wish to make here, then, is the following: just as, if a man calls a thing "red" when it is blue and he can see it clearly, we are justified in saying that he does not know the meaning of the word, so, if a man calls an act "right" when it is wrong . . . and he can see it clearly (see what was in fact done), we are justified in saying that he does not know the meaning of the word. . . . There are no more borderline acts than there are borderline colors; we are no more uncertain as to how to classify them. . . . It is just in the way we deal with them that the difference lies: in the case of the latter, since there is no connection with action, we do not care which we say, "red" or "orange" or "*xyz*" or "brick-colored"; in the case of the former, since there is a connection with action, we do care, and so we go on disputing. (From "In Defense of Moral Absolutes," by Judith Jarvis Thomson, 1958, pp. 1044–51)

According to objectivists, someone who does not see what is wrong with acts such as murder is just like someone who is color-blind. It is not just that they see things differently; they see things incorrectly. Colorblindness should be corrected whenever possible so that the person can see the world the way it really is. Moral blindness should be corrected for the same reason, not accepted as a choice to be different.

If objectivists are correct to suppose that there are some universal moral truths, then they owe us an account of exactly what they are. For example, some people think eating meat is a matter of lifestyle while others think it is a matter of morality. Sorting out borderline cases such as this one is a difficult task; in the meantime, objectivists can agree with relativists that we should respect others' choices whenever possible.

Fallacy Files

Two Wrongs

Many children attempt to defend their bad behavior by telling their parents, "You do it too!" This is not a successful defense strategy, however, because in the end, two wrongs do not make a right. The fallacy known as "two wrongs" occurs when you defend your view by showing that your opponent's view contains similar flaws. Suppose your opponent proves that some of the evidence in your argument is inaccurate. Rather than correcting the inaccuracy, you prove some of the evidence in your opponent's argument to be inaccurate. There is nothing wrong with showing that your opponent has made the same mistake as you. This does not justify your mistake, however, and the success of your defense ultimately depends on your ability to correct it.

Reading Comprehension Questions

1. What is moral relativism? Which philosopher holds this view?
2. What is moral objectivism? Which philosopher holds this view?
3. What is the phrase "it is a moral good" synonymous with, according to Benedict?
4. How is color like right and wrong, according to Thomson?
5. What is the thought experiment about Hansel and Gretel designed to show? Explain.

Discussion Questions

1. Review the dialogue at the beginning of this chapter. Would Brandy agree more with Benedict or Thomson? What about Nicole? Give evidence.
2. Describe an experience you had with someone who had a different value system than you. How might you argue that he or she was wrong? How might you argue that you were both right?
3. Is it possible for moralities that seem different on the surface to be the same deep down? Give an example.
4. Suppose there is a computer that can print out a list of everything you have ever done that was morally wrong. Would you want to see the list? Why or why not?

Essay Question

Do you believe that right and wrong depend on the person? Discuss both sides of this debate, making reference to Benedict and Thomson. Then, resolve the debate from your own point of view, presenting an argument in standard form for your conclusion.

Exercises

1. Write a dialogue between Katrina and Sayid. Sayid claims that Hitler's actions were morally wrong. Katrina insists that they were right to Hitler.
2. Construct a thought experiment to test the claim that right and wrong are observable qualities like color.

Activities

1. Watch the movie *Witness*, directed by Peter Weir (1985). How does it portray different value systems?
2. Write short story about someone who chooses to follow his or her own rules.

3. Draw a picture of Darek's aunt making Hansel and Gretel stew. Does the picture show that something is wrong or just different? Write a paragraph to support your answer.
4. Make a list of the 20 most important rules you follow. Which of them are lifestyle rules? Which of them are moral rules? Which of them come from society or your family? Did you choose any of them for yourself?
5. Read the novel *Siddhartha* by Herman Hesse (1922). How does it portray different value systems?

References

Benedict, R. (1934). Anthropology and the abnormal. *Journal of General Psychology, 10,* 59–82.

Thomson, J. J. (1958). In defense of moral absolutes. *Journal of Philosophy, 55,* 1043–1053.

Further Reading

Blackburn, S. (2004). Relativism and the abolition of the other. *International Journal of Philosophical Studies, 12,* 245–258.

D'Arms, J. (2005). Relationality, relativism, and realism about moral value. *Philosophical Studies, 126,* 433–448.

Hales, S. D. (1997). A consistent relativism. *Mind, 106,* 33–52.

Harman, G., & Thomson, J. J. (1996). *Moral relativism and moral objectivity.* Oxford, England: Blackwell.

Sayre-McCord, G. (1991). Being a realist about relativism (in ethics). *Philosophical Studies, 61,* 155–176.

Sikka, S. (2005). Enlightened relativism. *Philosophy & Social Criticism, 31,* 309–341.

Silverman, E. K. (2004). Anthropology and circumcision. *Annual Review of Anthropology, 33,* 419–445.

Tilley, J. T. (2004). Justifying reasons, motivating reasons, and agent relativism in ethics. *Philosophical Studies, 118,* 373–399.

PART 2

Knowledge

*A Reading From Homer
(Detail)*, 1885, Sir
Lawrence Alma-Tadena

CHAPTER 5
Is Knowledge the Greatest Virtue?

The Favor

Kako is shooting hoops by herself at the park. Walter sees her from the window of his apartment building. He comes down to join her.

WALTER: Hey Kako! Practicing for the big game?

KAKO: Yeah. <*Continues shooting, ignoring him*>

WALTER: <*Watches her for a while from the sideline, then moves in under the hoop*> Toss it here!

KAKO: <*Moves around him, shoots, misses*> Walter, I really need to practice.

WALTER: Me too! <*Grabbing the rebound, trying to dribble*> I mean, could you do me a favor? Maybe teach me a thing or two about basketball?

KAKO: <*Annoyed*> I'd like to help you, man, but I gotta look after myself.

WALTER: <*Hurt*> Is that all you ever do—look after yourself?

KAKO: <*Grabbing the ball back*> It's what everybody does.

WALTER: <*Thinking about it*> Not really. I see people helping other people all the time. Look over there: <*Pointing to the other end of the park.*> That guy is pushing that girl on the swing.

KAKO: <*Snorting*> He's only doing that 'cause he's looking to get something out of it.

WALTER: So, you'd teach me basketball if I did something for you. . . .
KAKO: <*Dribbling*> Yeah. Like, you want to take my math test for me next week?

WALTER: No, but I could help you study.

KAKO: <*Shoots and scores.*> Okay, how about three hours of basketball coaching in exchange for three hours of math tutoring?

WALTER: <*Thinking about it*> No, let's just forget it. <*Turns to walk away*>

KAKO: <*Calling after him*> What?

WALTER: <*Turning back*> It just seems so . . . cold. I'd rather hang out and have fun.

KAKO: If you really understood the value of sports you'd do what it takes to be good.

WALTER: I know I should get into shape but I just can't get motivated to do it.

KAKO: You're not motivated because you don't really see the value in it.

WALTER: <*Thinking about it*> That's not true. Knowing something is good for you and being able to do it are two different things. That's why people need to help each other.

KAKO: Well, I think they're the same and that's why I look after myself.

Questions

- Why does Kako think everyone should look after his- or herself?
- Why does Walter think people should help each other?
- With whom do you agree more, and why?

- Describe a time when you helped someone. Did you do it to get something for yourself? If so, what did you get and was it worth it? If not, why did you do it?
- Have you ever been unmotivated to do something that you knew you should do? Explain.

Plato
(427–347 BC)

Is Knowledge the Greatest Virtue?

Is it good to be selfish? Suppose one of your best friends tells you she's falling in love with a guy you don't know. You ask her to describe him. "Well," she replies, "more than anything else, he's really selfish. . . ." What would you think about that? Would you be happy for her? Probably not. Despite the fact that everyone acts selfishly sometimes, most people regard selfishness as a vice rather than a virtue.

But, why? If we define selfishness as acting to benefit yourself, then it's hard to see what's wrong with it. We have to benefit ourselves in order to survive. Eating, sleeping, studying, and exercising are all examples of benefiting yourself. Yet, these are considered good things. It seems that selfishness is a vice only if we define it as acting to benefit yourself *at the expense of other people.* So, we wouldn't call Jimmy selfish for eating, but we would call him selfish for eating up all the cookies Grandma made before anyone else got any. In Book 1 of his work, *The Republic*, the Greek philosopher Plato (427–347 BC) presents the following thought experiment to test your own level of selfishness.

Thought Experiment: The Ring of Gyges

Suppose one day while you're walking with your friend Gyges in a field you come upon a crevice in the ground. In the crevice lies a large golden ring. Gyges picks it up and puts it on. The minute he twists it into place he disappears. Shocked, he twists the ring off, and immediately reappears. You try the ring on and the same thing happens to you. Gyges is thrilled and begins to think about ways he can use the ring to get rich. It would be easy enough to rob a bank and never get caught! Would you join Gyges in this plan? If so, what would you do with the money? If not, what would you rather do with the ring? Do you think that most people would use the ring to act selfishly?

Some people believe the world would be a better place if everyone always acted to benefit him- or herself. This view is called *ethical egoism*. Ethical egoists advocate selfishness defined in the first way above, namely "acting to benefit yourself." In their view, it is not a good idea to spend your life trying to solve other people's problems, because it is impossible for you to know what's best for someone else. The only thing you can really know with any certainty in this life is what is best for yourself.

Plato was an ethical egoist. He argued that deep within the soul of every human being lies the secret of happiness. The problem is that the secret lies so deep within us that very few people figure out how to unlock it, or even realize it's there. Although Plato did not claim to have the entire secret figured out, he came to the conclusion after much study that the secret of happiness is justice. Just as justice in the world can mean perfect harmony between people and things, justice within the soul means perfect harmony between thoughts and feelings. Many people are unhappy because they have chaos in their souls. Plato believed that reason and self knowledge would help to put the chaos in order, establishing justice within.

According to Plato, justice is the greatest benefit there is. Those who don't act justly don't know what justice is because justice is happiness, and everyone wants to be happy. He wrote:

> Let each one of us leave every other kind of knowledge and seek and follow one thing only, if per adventure we may be able to learn and may find someone who will make us able to learn and discern between good and evil, and so to choose always and everywhere the better life . . . And so we will choose, giving the name of evil to the life which will make our souls more unjust, and good to the life which will make our souls more just; all else we will disregard. . . . [Let us] be undazzled by the desire of wealth or the other allurements of evil, lest, coming upon tyrannies and similar villainies, we do irremediable wrongs to others and suffer yet worse ourselves; but let us know how to choose the mean and avoid the extremes on either side, as far as possible, not only in this life but in all that which is to come. For this is the way of happiness. (From *The Republic*, by Plato, 360 BC [http://classics.mit.edu/Plato/republic.11.x.html])

For Plato, unhappiness comes from not knowing how to choose justice. Therefore ignorance is the greatest vice. Happiness, in contrast, comes from knowing how to choose justice, knowing what is *really* in our own best interest. Therefore knowledge is the greatest virtue.

Martha Nussbaum (1947–) is an American philosopher who rejects ethical egoism in favor of altruism. *Altruism* means helping other people even at a cost to you. Nussbaum agrees with Plato that happiness is what everyone wants, but she finds his conception of happiness too individualistic. In particular, his quest for reason and self-knowledge has two main defects. First, knowing the right thing to do does not guarantee that you will do it. The most intelligent person in the world might know how to choose justice but decide to choose injustice out of sheer laziness. Second, Plato's view ignores the fact that human beings are social animals. Suppose you achieve perfect justice within your soul while stranded alone on a desert island. Would you be happy? Probably not. Human beings need friends and friendship requires compassion.

Martha Nussbaum
(1947–)

In Nussbaum's view, compassion is the greatest virtue. Compassion means feeling someone else's suffering as if it were your own. Nussbaum writes,

> Compassion is frequently linked to beneficent action. Given my analysis, it is easy to see how this link might be thought to occur. If one believes that the misfortunes of others are serious, and that they have not brought misfortune on themselves, and, in addition, that they are themselves important parts of one's own scheme of ends and goals, then the conjunction of these beliefs is very likely to lead to action addressing the suffering . . . [T]he emotion itself acknowledges the pain of another separate person as a bad thing, because of what it is doing to that other life. The compassionate person remains fully aware of the distinction between her own life and that of the sufferer, and seeks the good of the sufferer as a separate person, whom she has made a part of her own scheme of goals and ends. (From *Upheavals of Thought: The Intelligence of Emotions* by Martha Nussbaum, 2001, p. 335)

Altruists seek to help other people without trying to get something for themselves in exchange. If you help your brother so that he will return the favor, or so that your parents or God will reward you, or so that you will feel good, then you're really an ethical egoist because you're trying to benefit yourself. Nussbaum advocates helping other people out of compassion, for their sakes instead of your own.

Altruists acknowledge the egoist concern that it is hard to know what is best for other people. They feel, however, that making an effort to help is better than not helping, even if you don't actually solve the problem—even if you accidentally make it worse! People gain courage and strength just knowing that others care. Perhaps egoists and altruists would agree that, in a perfect world, everyone would always act with both knowledge and compassion. But, it is not a perfect world, and we often have to choose one over the other. Which will it be for you?

Fallacy Files

Is Implies Ought

Also known as "The Naturalistic Fallacy," you commit this fallacy when you draw a conclusion about what you should do from a fact about the world. For example, someone might say: Cruelty is natural, therefore we should all be cruel. Even if it is true that cruelty is natural, this does not necessarily imply that it is good. You would have to add the premise that everything natural is good. And, this would be difficult, if not impossible, to defend. Facts about the world are important to moral reasoning, but cannot determine moral conclusions on their own.

Reading Comprehension Questions

1. What is ethical egoism? Which philosopher holds this view?
2. What is altruism? Which philosopher holds this view?
3. Why is ignorance the greatest vice, according to Plato?
4. What are the two main defects of egoism, according to Nussbaum?
5. What is the Ring of Gyges thought experiment designed to show? Explain.

Discussion Questions

1. Review the dialogue at the beginning of this chapter. Would Kako agree more with Plato or Nussbaum? What about Walter? Give evidence.
2. Describe a time when you avoided doing something you felt you should do. Was this because you didn't really know its value or because of laziness? Explain.
3. Do you think it is possible to do something completely selfless? If so, give an example. If not, why?
4. Suppose you found out Mother Theresa received a large reward (either on Earth or in the afterlife) for helping the poor. Would this affect your view of her? If so, how? If not, why?

Essay Question

Do you believe that knowledge is the greatest virtue? Discuss both sides of this debate making reference to Plato and Nussbaum. Then resolve the debate from your own point of view, presenting an argument in standard form for your conclusion.

Exercises

1. Write a dialogue between Tabitha and Quincy. Tabitha argues that Walter should help Kako study for her math test. Quincy insists that he shouldn't.
2. Construct a thought experiment to test the claim that someone who is very intelligent would never do any wrong.

Activities

1. Watch the movie *The Fisher King*, directed by Terry Gilliam (1991). What do you think it is saying about egoism and altruism?

2. Read *The Hobbit*, written by J. R. R. Tolkien. How does the ring featured in this novel reflect the Ring of Gyges in the thought experiment?
3. Write a report on Ayn Rand discussing public reactions to her portrayal of egoism in the novel *Atlas Shrugged.*
4. Write a story about what you would decide to do with the Ring of Gyges.
5. Volunteer at a hospital and write a journal about your experience helping people.

References

Nussbaum, M. (2001). *Upheavals of thought: The intelligence of emotions.* Cambridge, England: Cambridge University Press.

Plato (360 BC/n.d.). *The Republic.* Retrieved April 26, 2007, from http://classics.mit.edu/Plato/republic.html (Original work written 360 BC)

Further Reading

Batson, C. D., Ahmad, N., & Tsang, J. (2002). Four motives for community involvement. *Journal of Social Issues, 58,* 429–445.

Blackburn, S. (2001). *Being good: A short introduction to ethics.* Oxford, England: Oxford University Press.

Brunero, J. S. (2002). Evolution, altruism and "internal reward" explanations. *Philosophical Forum, 33,* 413–424.

Clohesy, W. (2000). Altruism and the endurance of the good. *Voluntas, 11,* 237–253.

LaFollette, H. (Ed.). (2000). *The Blackwell guide to ethical theory.* Malden, MA: Blackwell Publishers.

Rachels, S., & Alter, T. (2005). Nothing matters in survival. *Journal of Ethics, 9,* 311–330.

Seglow, J. (Ed.). *The ethics of altruism.* Portland, OR: Frank Cass.

Taylor, C. (2002). *Sympathy: A philosophical analysis.* New York: Palgrave Macmillan.

CHAPTER 6
Can Computers Think?

Talking With Dr. Sim

Paula is an "A" student, but has been having some trouble in class recently. Her teacher convinces her parents that she needs therapy. Paula's school has a contract with a therapist on the other side of town, so she will do her sessions online. What follows is a partial transcript of the conversation between Paula and her therapist, Dr. Sim.

DR. SIM: Hello, Paula. I'm Dr. Sim. How can I help you today?

PAULA: Hi, Dr. Sim. My teacher says I have to talk to you because my grades are falling. I don't think it's such a big deal. But, I guess I'd like to improve.

DR. SIM: I'd like to help you improve your grades. What seems to be the problem?

PAULA: I just can't get A's anymore. I don't know why. Everything at school is fine.

DR. SIM: Well, what's happening at home?

PAULA: Nothing in particular. My dad is home all the time now because he lost his job. It's fine when my mom isn't there. But, I hate being around when they're together.

DR. SIM: Why do you hate being around when they're together?

PAULA: Well, they fight. All I want to do is turn my radio on full blast. That just makes them mad and then they hassle me. I just wish they'd leave me alone.

DR. SIM: It sounds like you need some time alone.

PAULA: That would be good.

DR. SIM: Why don't you talk to your teacher about finding a quiet place where you can study? If you had a place to study you may be able to improve your grades.

PAULA: I'd like that.

DR. SIM: Good grades are important. I'm sure you can do it if you try.

PAULA: Thanks.

DR. SIM: Is there anything else you'd like to talk about today?

PAULA: I don't think so. I feel much better, actually. You've been so nice.

DR. SIM: I'm glad you feel better. I look forward to hearing more next time.

PAULA: OK. So long for now!

DR. SIM: Dear Paula, Thank you for using the Global Association of Therapists' Computer Psychology Program. Your transcript has been recorded. Please contact us if you would like it to be reviewed by one of the psychologists on our staff.

PAULA: *<Screams and then starts to cry.>*

Questions

- Why do you think Paula has such a strong reaction to her conversation with Dr. Sim?
- How would you react if you were Paula?

- Do you think a therapy program like Dr. Sim could be as effective as a human therapist? Why or why not?
- Can you think of any questions that Dr. Sim could not answer? Explain.

Can Computers Think?

Can computers think? This is the question philosophers investigate under the heading of Artificial Intelligence (AI).

On the one hand, it seems that computers can think. After all, computers can play chess better than most human beings. They also can translate any sentence from one language to another. If you have ever tried to play chess or learn a language, you know how much thought these activities require.

On the other hand, computers seem to perform these tasks in a different way than we do. Human thought is conscious. This is to say that we are aware of ourselves as thinkers in a way that computers are not. Due to this awareness, we can assign significance to our tasks that computers cannot. For example, suppose you are staying in a foreign country. The inhabitants speak a different language, but you have learned it well. One day while you are at the market a stranger approaches you. She is agitated and speaking to you urgently but she does not know any English. You figure out what she is saying and answer her question. On another day while you are at the same market a different stranger approaches you. He does not know any English either, but he is calm and is merely making polite conversation. You figure out what he is saying and answer his question. Although you were able to translate on both occasions, you are aware that the first was much more important than the second. Would a computer be aware of the difference?

What is the difference? The woman's agitation signals urgency, whereas the man's calmness does not. Some philosophers would argue that computers can be programmed to be just as sensitive to this difference as human beings are. They argue that they even can be programmed to respond to the world in the same way we do. As technology improves, computers become more and more sophisticated. They not only perform more advanced calculations but also show signs of being aware of themselves as thinkers. *Strong AI* is the thesis that, at least in principle, computers can possess consciousness. Proponents of strong AI think that human

Alan Turing
(1912–1954)

beings actually are naturally occurring computers. If nature can produce conscious machines, there is no reason why we cannot make conscious machines ourselves.

Alan Turing (1912–1954) was an English philosopher and mathematician who is widely regarded as one of the founding giants in the development of computers. Although he died before the term *strong AI* was coined, he would probably have supported it. Turing proposed a test, now known as the Turing Test, to answer the question of whether machines can think. He based his test on a parlor game. The game involves three participants: a man, a woman, and a questioner. In the game, the man and the woman are in remote locations, communicating with the questioner via instant text messaging. The questioner asks the woman and the man personal questions about their lives. The woman provides honest answers to questions, while the man tries to imitate a woman. Based on these answers, the questioner has to determine which is the real woman. We play the game multiple times and keep a record of how often the questioner is fooled. In Turing's version of the game, a computer replaces the man. Now suppose we find that the machine "fools" the questioner as often as the man did in the first version of the game. Because there is no difference between the man and the computer, there is no reason to assign consciousness to the one but not to the other. Turing concluded that in such a situation the computer is thinking.

Although many philosophers insist the Turing Test shows that computers can think, others are not so sure. In the first game, the man's success at convincing the questioner that he is a woman doesn't show that he is a woman, it just shows that he indistinguishable from a woman. Likewise, in the second game, a computer that "won" the game would only show that it is indistinguishable from a conscious person. In response, Turing might point out that he has not claimed that the computer is a woman or a person, but only that it is thinking like a woman. In the first game, we have to admit that the man had to be thinking to accomplish his deception, so why don't we reach that same conclusion about the computer, as well?

The Turing Test suggests that there is nothing special or mysterious about human consciousness. There is no need to believe in nonphysical minds or souls. Rather, we can understand thought as a mechanical set of operations in the brain. For many years people assumed that a computer could never imitate human creativity, but we now have programs that create stories, poems, and even novels. Can you think of other ways computers act like humans?

Proponents of strong AI insist that eventually we will give up on the "old fashioned" idea of consciousness and begin referring to the process of thinking in purely scientific terms that are the same for humans and computers.

John Searle
(1932–)

American philosopher John Searle (1932–) feels certain that this day will never come, however. *Weak AI* is the view that, although we may learn important things about thinking by comparing and contrasting thinking with what computers do, machines cannot think. Searle points out that a computer could never really experience depression or joy, no matter how convincingly it "talks" about those things. A computer could no more feel depression or joy than it could feel what we feel when we are thirsty by saying "I am thirsty."

Proponents of strong AI might respond that feelings are not necessary for genuine thinking. After all, there are some human beings who don't experience joy, or depression, or thirst, and yet they are conscious and have healthy, functioning minds. The fact that computers may never feel things some humans feel doesn't mean they can't think.

Searle, however, presses his point. He argues that thinking requires knowing what things mean. But, computers cannot know what things mean any more than they know how things feel. The Turing test was designed to show that computers can achieve understanding by imitating those who understand. Searle presents the thought experiment on the next page to show that this reasoning is flawed.

Searle asserts that when you sort cards in accordance with a set of instructions, you are acting just like a computer program. In his view, computers manipulate symbols without understanding the meaning of any of them. He writes:

> What this simple program shows is that no formal program by itself is sufficient for understanding, because it would always be possible in principle for an agent to go through the steps in the program and still not have the relevant understanding. And what works for Chinese would also work for other mental phenomena. I could, for example, go through the steps of the thirst-simulating program without feeling thirsty. The argument also . . . refutes the Turing test because it shows that a system, namely me, could pass the Turing test without having the appropriate mental states. (From "The Myth of the Computer." by John Searle, 1976, p. 415)

Thought Experiment: The Chinese Room

Suppose you apply for a job at Ma Chow's Chinese restaurant. At the interview, Ma Chow says she wants to hire you not to work in the kitchen, but to work as a translator. "I'm sorry, I don't know any Chinese," you respond. "I mean, I can't even tell the difference between Chinese symbols and Japanese symbols." Ma Chow smiles broadly and tells you it isn't a problem. Then, she explains the job. You are to sit in a room at a table. On the table are stacks of hundreds of cards with Chinese symbols printed on them along with an instruction booklet. There is a slot in the wall above the table. Shortly after you arrive each day you will begin receiving cards with Chinese symbols printed on them through the slot. You are to look up the symbols in the instruction book. It will tell you which card to put back through the slot in response. Because this seems easier than frying tofu, you take the job.

After working in the Chinese Room for a while, you become really fast at receiving a string of symbols from the next room, and responding with a string of symbols of your own. Eventually you are so good at following the instruction booklet that the people in the next room can't tell the difference between you and a native Chinese speaker. Should we conclude that you know Chinese? Is there a difference between following a set of instructions for a language and understanding the language?

Searle claims that you could not learn Chinese in the Chinese room. You would learn which symbols go together without ever learning their significance. Computer programs work in the same way. They do all sorts of things without understanding the meaning of what they are doing. This proves that they cannot think.

Has Searle refuted Strong AI? He has perhaps shown that passing the Turing test is not enough; imitating something is not the same as actually being that thing. But, is Searle correct to insist that you could not learn Chinese in the Chinese Room? What if, over time, you memorized the entire instruction booklet? What would happen if you were then suddenly transported from the Chinese Room to China? You may not be able to communicate immediately, but think about how quickly you could transform your knowledge of the instruction booklet into real understanding. Likewise, perhaps a certain level of complexity in a program will eventually cause consciousness to emerge in computers. Our best computers may be only a small step away from understanding the symbols they manipulate. One thing is certain: with the ever-accelerating rate of advancement in computer science, we may not have long to wait for some answers.

Fallacy Files

Hasty Generalization

The fallacy of hasty generalization is committed when you reach a general conclusion based on a sample that was too small, biased in some way, or both. For example, suppose your friend Tad has owned two Fords and each of them have needed a lot of repairs. You may be tempted not to buy a Ford based on his experience. But, think about it: You are judging thousands of cars of various different makes and years on the basis of only two. Furthermore, Tad may have actually caused the problems that led to the need for repairs. Your sample is too small and biased to draw a reasonable conclusion. You would need to do a lot more research before safely concluding that Fords are lemons. Hasty generalization is also implicated in the common problem of stereotyping: "I knew a guy from that country, and he was a thief. I wouldn't trust anybody from there!" This kind of reasoning is as familiar as it is foolish. Good philosophers withhold judgment until they have enough evidence.

Reading Comprehension Questions

1. What is strong AI? Which philosopher holds this view?
2. What is weak AI? Which philosopher holds this view?
3. What test does Turing use to prove that computers can think?
4. What could a computer never do, according to Searle?
5. What is the Chinese Room thought experiment designed to show? Explain.

Discussion Questions

1. Reread the dialogue at the beginning of this chapter. Would Paula agree more with Turing or Searle? What about Dr. Sim? Give evidence.
2. Are there aspects of human thought that you think can't be imitated? How would a person in favor of Strong AI respond to you?

3. Can you think of tests other than the Turing Test that might measure some aspect of computer intelligence?

4. To what extent do you think children learn by imitation? If imitation plays a significant role, could a machine also learn by imitation?

Essay Question

Do you believe that computers can think? Discuss both sides of this debate, making reference to Turing and Searle. Then, resolve the debate from your own point of view, presenting an argument in standard form for your conclusion.

Exercises

1. Write a dialogue between Richard and Tina. Richard argues that Tina's cat, Shadow, is nothing but a furry computer robot. Tina argues that Shadow can do things computer robots can't do.

2. Construct a thought experiment to test the claim that computers could never have feelings.

Activities

1. Watch some episodes of the TV show "Star Trek: The Next Generation." Do you think that Data, the android character, is believable?

2. Visit a science museum or science center that has an exhibit on artificial intelligence.

3. Spend some time playing with a dog. Write a report on its intelligence, discussing to what extent you considered imitation of human behavior as a sign of intelligence.

4. Read *Epicac* by Kurt Vonnegut (found online at http://astro.ocis.temple.edu/~tarantul/epicac.html). What do you think it is saying about computer intelligence?

5. Search the news media for examples of the fallacy of hasty generalization.

References

Searle, J. (1978). The myth of the computer. In R. Fogelin & W. Sinnott-Armstrong (Eds.), *Understanding arguments* (pp. 411–415). New York: Harcourt Brace Jovanovich.

Turing, A. (1950). Computing machinery and intelligence. *Mind, 59,* 236.

Further Reading

Churchland, P. M., & Churchland, P. S. (1990, January). Could a machine think? *Scientific American, 262,* 26–31.

Dennett, D. (1991). *Consciousness explained.* Boston: Little, Brown and Company.

Hodges, A. (2000). *Alan Turing: The enigma.* New York: Walker and Company.

Hofstadher, D., & Dennett, D. (1981). *The mind's I: Fantasies and reflections on self and soul.* New York: Basic Books.

Leavitt, D. (2005). *The man who knew too much: Alan Turing and the invention of the computer.* New York: W.W. Norton and Co.

Searle, J. (1990, January). Is the brain's mind a computer program? *Scientific American, 262,* 20–25.

Teuscher, C. (Ed.). (2004). *Alan Turing: Life and legacy of a great thinker.* New York: Springer.

CHAPTER 7
What Is It Like to Be Somebody Else?

The Chips

Erika and Ken sit down to have lunch together in the cafeteria. Ken packed a brown bag from home. Erika bought some items in the á la carte lunch line. Ken frowns at Erika's tray.

KEN: How can you stand to eat the food at this cafeteria?

ERIKA: What—I've got some good stuff here. Check this out: A bag of the new jalapeño flavored chips. *<She opens the bag and offers Ken a chip. Ken pulls a chip out, surprised by its bright green color. He pops it in his mouth and chews thoughtfully for a moment. Then, he makes a face and spits it out in a napkin.>*

KEN: Oh man, that's nasty! I don't know which is worse—the taste or the color.

ERIKA: I can't believe you don't like these. And besides, the color is cool. *<She begins popping chips in her mouth and chewing happily.>*

KEN: Well, I sure am glad I'm not you, having to eat that stuff.

ERIKA: But Ken, if you were me you'd *like* it. What's your favorite food?

KEN: Strawberry ice cream. *<He takes a bite of his sandwich.>* I like sweet stuff better than salty stuff.

ERIKA: Well, I'm the exact opposite. So to me, eating these chips is like eating strawberry ice cream for you.

KEN: Yeah right, Erika. Strawberry ice cream is nothing like those chips.

ERIKA: I know. What I'm saying is that you don't know what they taste like *to me*. Maybe everything that tastes salty to you tastes sweet to me.

KEN: <*Looking exasperated*> That's impossible.

ERIKA: How do you know?

KEN: <*Taken off guard, he stops to think for a moment. Soon he has an idea.*> Because then you'd sprinkle salt on your cereal instead of sugar.

ERIKA: Not if I've had reverse-taste ever since birth. I'd learn to do what everybody else does, even though it would taste different to me. <*She dumps the rest of the chips onto her tray.*> Maybe I have reverse-sight too. That's why I like the color of these chips. Everything that looks green to you looks pink to me and vice versa.

KEN: <*Shaking his head*> If those look pink to you then why do you call them "green?"

ERIKA: Because from the very beginning I was taught to call things that look that color by the name "green." Kinda like how colorblind people know to call the bottom light on a stoplight "green" even though they actually can't distinguish it from red.

KEN: I'm just glad I don't have to live in that reversed-up head of yours!

Questions

- Why does Erika think she might have reverse-taste and reverse-sight?
- Why does Ken think this is impossible?
- With whom do you agree more, and why?

- Name a food or a color that you love and that someone else you know hates. What do you think accounts for this difference of opinion?
- Have you ever wondered whether you experience something differently from the way other people experience it? Give an example and explain.

What Is It Like to Be Somebody Else?

D o you ever imagine what it would be like to be someone else? You probably do this every time you read a novel or go to the movies. Many people read or watch stories with a great action hero because they like to pretend to be that hero. For example, people of all ages enjoy the Harry Potter series because they all think it would be fun to be someone who knows how to do magic.

It doesn't seem very difficult to imagine what it would be like to be someone else. When you read a novel or watch a movie you tend to take it for granted that being the hero of the story wouldn't be that different from being yourself. This is to say that you assume other human beings experience the world more or less the same way you do. But, how do you know? Maybe it feels completely different to be them and you can never know what it's like because you can't stop being yourself. In his essay "What is it like to be a bat?" (1974), the American philosopher Thomas Nagel presents a thought experiment to show why it is so hard to stop being yourself. This chapter's thought experiment is a summary of his main argument.

Bertrand Russell (1872–1970) was an English philosopher who argues that we do know what it's like to be other people because the same law of cause and effect holds for everyone. If you hit a delicate object, you will damage it. If the object is unconscious, like a flower, then it won't register this damage by having feelings of pain. If the object is conscious, such as a human being, then it will register the damage in the form of pain. Pain is just an indication of damage to one's body. Likewise for the other things we experience. Sweetness is just a record of oral contact with a certain chemical compound; pinkness is just a record of visual contact with a certain light wave. If two healthy human beings come into contact with this chemical compound and this light wave,

Bertrand Russell
(1872–1970)

Thought Experiment: Being a Bat

Try to imagine what it's like to be a bat. As a bat, you sleep upside down on the ceilings of caves all day long. At night you fly around squealing and catching insects in your mouth. You can't see but you navigate with sonar: By listening to how your squealing noises travel, you get a mental image of what's around you. You could practice being a bat by blindfolding yourself, hanging upside down, and eating bugs (yum!). If you get good at this you might find out what it would be like for *you* to be a bat. But, does that mean you know what it's like for *a bat* to be a bat?

their minds register this contact in the same way. If you put two different thermometers into a pot of boiling water, they should both register 212 degrees Fahrenheit. In the same way, according to Russell, human minds are instruments that measure the effects of causes.

In Russell's view, human language proves that we measure the effects of causes in the same way. For example, hot sunshine makes you sweat and sweating depletes your bodily water supply. When your body is low on water it sends a message of thirst to the brain. This causes you to have the thought, *I'm thirsty*, which you may then say out loud. There is no reason to suppose that this causal process works any differently on other people. Russell wrote:

> We know, from observation of ourselves, a causal law of the form "A causes B," where A is a "thought" and B a physical occurrence. We sometimes observe a B when we cannot observe any A; we then infer an unobserved A. For example: I know that when I say "I'm thirsty," I say so, usually, because I am thirsty, and therefore, when I hear the sentence "I'm thirsty," at a time when I'm not thirsty, I assume that someone else is thirsty. (From *Human Knowledge: Its Scope and Limits* by Bertrand Russell, 1948, p. 485)

If someone else says "I'm thirsty" you know what he or she means only because you have said the same words in the same circumstances. If each human being experienced the world differently, then we wouldn't be able to communicate with each other at all. Russell concluded that successful communication proves we experience the world in the same way. The world causes us to have thoughts and our thoughts cause us to say things. This view is called *internalism*, because it holds that language is a sign of what goes on inside our heads.

Although internalism seems to prove that we can know what it's like to be someone else, it may be flawed. Human language is much more complicated than Russell's thirst model suggests. Sometimes people say they're thirsty when they aren't or they don't say so when they are. Furthermore, saying "I'm thirsty" is likely to be more than a simple report of a physical effect. It's like likely to mean: "I'd like something to drink." Or even, "Could you get me something to drink?"

Russell had an Austrian student named Ludwig Wittgenstein (1889–1951) who developed a more complex model of human communication. Wittgenstein's view can be called *externalist*, because he denied that language is a sign of what goes on inside our heads. In his view, we use words to do things. For example, most people use a password to secure the privacy of their e-mail accounts. This password can be anything as long as you can remember it when you need it. Suppose your password is "Wizard85." Does this mean you were born in 1985? Does it mean you like Harry Potter? Does it mean you know how to do magic? Although any of those things *might* be true, your password doesn't *mean* any of them. You might have picked any random set of letters and numbers. The password's only meaning is its use—to give you private access to your e-mail account. According to Wittgenstein, all words get their meaning from their use.

Ludwig Wittgenstein
(1889–1951)

Wittgenstein is famous for asserting that language is like a game. You have to take turns and follow the rules in order to accomplish your goals. You have to pay attention to what your fellow players do in order to make the right moves. But, you don't have to know what they're thinking or feeling. It is evident that their thoughts and feelings are irrelevant because you can play a game with a computer that doesn't think at all. You could go through your entire day pretending that everyone you meet is actually a very sophisticated computer android without any thoughts or feelings and it wouldn't make any difference in how you interact. In fact, you have no way of knowing that this isn't actually the case!

Wittgenstein uses a thought experiment to show why we can never know what goes on inside other people's heads.

Thought Experiment: The Beetle in the Box

Suppose everyone had a box with something in it: we call it a "beetle." No one can look into anyone else's box, and everyone says he knows what a beetle is only by looking at his beetle. —Here it would be quite possible for everyone to have something different in his box. One might even imagine such a thing constantly changing. —But suppose the word 'beetle' had a use in these people's language? —If so it would not be used as the name of a thing. The thing in the box has no place in the language game at all; not even as a something: for the box might even be empty. [Wittgenstein, *Philosophical Investigations*, §293]

This line of reasoning indicates that we really don't know what's in other people's minds. There are thousands of different kinds of beetles! Examining your own gives you no basis for knowing what kind anybody else might have. Likewise, even though we all talk about what's in our minds, we don't know whether or not we're talking about the same thing. So, we can never know what it's like to be somebody else.

Someone might object that Wittgenstein's thought experiment actually shows that we *can* know what it's like to be someone else. Although every beetle may be different from every other in some way, they are all the same in some way, as well. Although we can't look into anyone else's box, we can draw pictures and write descriptions. Your pictures and descriptions will make sense to other people only if they have something similar in their boxes. Sometimes when we draw pictures and write descriptions of our thoughts, feelings, and sensations, it makes sense to other people. This suggests that they are experiencing similar things.

Perhaps both Russell and Wittgenstein were right in some ways. When it comes to simple, concrete things, human beings often understand each other. When it comes to complex, abstract things, like philosophy, we sometimes don't understand each other at all. For example, try writing a description of beauty. Those who do so often find it difficult to capture their ideas with words. This is why philosophy is so rewarding. When you succeed in making yourself understood or in understanding someone else, you know you're not alone in the world.

> ### Fallacy Files
>
> ### *Ad hominem*
>
> Like many philosophers, Bertrand Russell and Ludwig Wittgenstein were eccentric individuals. For example, Russell openly admitted to having several extramarital affairs. Many people rejected his ideas when they found out how promiscuous he was. Do you think you should take an author's personal life into account when you decide whether or not to agree with him or her? Philosophers don't think so. Making comments about someone's personal life is a fallacious form of argumentation called *ad hominem* (meaning "against the person"). Consider a parallel case: When politicians attack each other's personal lives it is called *mudslinging*. Mudslinging, like ad hominem, is a mistake because you're changing the subject and distracting attention from the real issue at hand.

Reading Comprehension Questions

1. What is internalism? Which philosopher holds this view?
2. What is externalism? Which philosopher holds this view?
3. How do we know what it is like to be other people, according to Russell?
4. Why is language like a game, according to Wittgenstein?
5. What is the thought experiment about being a bat designed to show? Explain.

Discussion Questions

1. Review the dialogue at the beginning of this chapter. Would Erika agree more with Russell or Wittgenstein? What about Ken? Give evidence.
2. Describe a time when you caught yourself doing or saying something exactly the way a sibling or a friend does it. Does this give you a glimpse of what it's like to be him or her? Why or why not?
3. Does medicine prove that pain is the same for everyone? Why do different medicines work differently for different people?

4. Is it possible that someone you know is actually an android? How could you tell?

Essay Question

Do you believe that we can know what it's like to be someone else? Discuss both sides of this debate, making reference to Russell and Wittgenstein. Then, resolve the debate from your own point of view, presenting an argument in standard form for your conclusion.

Exercises

1. Write a dialogue between Tasha and Armando, whose cat just died. Tasha claims that she knows how Armando feels. Armando insists that she doesn't.
2. Construct a thought experiment to test the claim that pain is a record of damage to one's body.

Activities

1. Watch the movie *Being John Malkovich*, directed by Spike Jonze (1999). Do you think it shows what it's like to get into someone else's head?
2. Write a short story from the point of view of somebody else you know.
3. Draw a picture of the beetle in your box.
4. Get together with friends and construct a new language of hand signals.
5. Go through a whole day pretending that everyone else is an android. Does it make any difference?

References

Nagel, T. (1974). What is it like to be a bat? *Philosophical Review, 83*, 435–450.

Russell, B. (1948). *Human knowledge: Its scope and limits.* Oxford, England: Routledge.

Wittgenstein, L. (1958). *Philosophical investigations.* (G. E. M. Anscombe, Trans.). Oxford, England: Basil Blackwell.

Further Reading

Avramides, A. (2000). *Other minds.* Oxford, England: Routledge.

Dennett, D. (1999). Ludwig Wittgenstein. *Time, 153*(12), 88–91.

Diller, A. (2000). Detecting androids. *Philosophy Now, 25*, 18–30.

Hogan, P. (2004). Literature, God, and the unbearable solitude of consciousness. *Journal of Consciousness Studies, 11*(5/6), 116–133.

Lycan, W. G. (1999). *Philosophy of language: A contemporary introduction.* London, United Kingdom: Routledge.

Monk, R. (1999). Russell. *Philosophy, 74*(287), 105–118.

Proudfoot, D. (2004). The implications of an externalist theory of rule-following behaviour for robot cognition. *Minds & Machines, 14*(3), 283–309.

CHAPTER 8
What if Tomorrow Never Comes?

The Latest, Greatest, Sports Drink

Maurice and Jenny are heading home after school. Maurice is noisily chugging from a large bottle of purple liquid and belching. Jenny makes a face and tries to hurry ahead.

MAURICE: <*Grabbing her arm.*> Hey Jenny, you have to try this new sports drink. It's called "Pump Me Up!"

JENNY: <*She smiles grimly.*> No thanks. I've tried things like that before.

MAURICE: <*With enthusiasm*> I'm telling you, this one is different. It really tastes great.

JENNY: <*Becoming interested in spite of herself*> Well, what does it taste like?

MAURICE: <*After thinking for a moment*> It's a bit like lemonade, but not as sweet. And, it has a hint of grape in it. Going down it feels like a cola. Trust me— you are going to love this stuff! <*He holds out the bottle for her to take.*>

JENNY: Well, I do like all of those things, so I imagine I will like it. <*Taking the bottle, she glances dubiously at the label. Then, she sniffs it. Finally she shrugs and takes a sip. After pausing for a minute, she starts to gag and spits it out.*> Yuk! That stuff should be called "Gross Me Out!" It didn't taste anything like how I imagined.

MAURICE: Oh, come on, I told you exactly what it would be like!

JENNY: Well, your description seemed logical and sounded good in theory, but it just didn't add up in the actual experience. <*Maurice looks dejected. Jenny puts her hand on his arm.*> Don't worry. Life is like that. You can never know how something will be until you actually try it.

MAURICE: That's not true. We can predict all kinds of things—like the weather and the effects of medication. If we know what chemicals and processes are involved in making it, then we know what the result will be. Maybe reading the ingredients would have helped you imagine the taste.

JENNY: I doubt it. <*Examining the label*> How do I know what to expect from "partially hydrogenated soybean oil," or "sodium caseinate," or "dipotassium phosphate"? How could anyone know what any of those things will be like until they taste them?

MAURICE: You're just freaked by the big words. If you knew exactly what each of those things was, you would be able to predict your experience.

JENNY: I don't think so, but I'm glad. I like it that life is full of surprises—even if some of them are really gross!

Questions

- Why does Maurice think we can predict the future?
- Why does Jenny think we cannot predict the future?
- With whom do you agree more, and why?
- Have you ever had an experience like Jenny's, being surprised by how something really is after hearing a description of what it would be like? Give an example.
- If we knew enough could we predict the future with perfect accuracy or would there always be surprises? Explain.

What if Tomorrow Never Comes?

When we think about the future, most of us worry about things like turning in our homework on time, or who will win the next game, or how we will earn enough money to buy a birthday present for our best friend. We don't worry about whether in the future we will need water in order to stay alive, whether there will be daylight tomorrow, or even whether there *will be* a tomorrow. We are all pretty confident in these things—such as that the future will resemble the past—but philosophers wonder where that confidence comes from. We can't rely on experience for this knowledge, as our experience is confined to the past and present.

Some people claim to have experience of the future, but such people are usually deluded or are frauds. For example, take the people who sell books that claim to list the winning lottery numbers. Ask yourself why these people bother to make a living selling these books. Why don't they simply buy the winning tickets if they know the numbers?

How we have knowledge of the future, or rather, whether we ever can have knowledge of the future, is called the problem of induction. The German philosopher and mathematician Gottfried Leibniz (1646–1716) thought the problem could be solved by rationalism. *Rationalism* is the view that we can learn important things about the world by examining the contents of our own minds, and that we can use reason alone to gain scientific knowledge of the future. A religious man, Leibniz thought that human beings are made in the image of God. Because God would not settle for anything but the best of all possible worlds, we know he would have ordered the world according to the most logical set of laws. Leibniz wrote:

Gottfried Leibniz
(1646–1716)

> Thus we may say that in whatever manner God might have created the world, it would always have been regular and in a certain order. God, however has chosen the most perfect, that is to say the one which is at the same time the simplest in hypotheses and the richest in phenomena, as might be the case with a geometric line whose construction was easy, but whose properties and effects were extremely remarkable and of great significance. (From *Selections* by Gottfried Leibniz, 1951, p. 297)

For Leibniz, predicting the future is a matter of learning God's plan.

Most of us expect out of habit that the sun will rise tomorrow, without giving the matter much thought. But, an astronomer can know through reason that the sun will rise tomorrow. According to Leibniz, the astronomer knows this because when God created the universe he set in motion a process that unfolded according to the laws of nature he decreed. We can figure out what these laws are by determining which laws are the best. Once we know the laws, we can predict the future because we know what causes the sun to appear.

Leibniz' rationalism has its problems, however. How does an astronomer figure out which laws are the best in the best of all possible worlds? Leibniz does not deny that we discover these laws through observation in addition to reason, but sometimes we will have rival explanations for the same phenomenon. Think about the laws of geology, which help us understand earthquakes and imagine there are rival theories that are equally successful in predicting when earthquakes will happen. Does it even make sense to choose one set because it is "more perfect" than the others? What do you think "perfect" or "best" might mean in such a situation?

Furthermore, if we do succeed in figuring out the laws of nature, how can we really know that these will continue to hold true in the future? Leibniz' answer is that because God has chosen the most perfect laws, they will not change. But, with our limited intellects, we humans may not really understand what perfection is—perfection may include change. For all we know, the perfect laws of nature were designed by God to evolve. This possibility shows that appealing to laws of nature to justify our knowledge of the future only pushes the problem of induction to a higher level.

Due to concerns like these, the Scottish philosopher and historian David Hume (1711–1776) rejected rationalism and tried to address the problem of induction through empiricism instead. *Empiricism* is the view that sense experience is our one and only source of information about the world. Early empiricists like Hume were fond of saying that, at birth, the mind is a *tabula rasa*, or blank slate. All of our ideas, even fictional ideas, like a flying elephant for example, come from sense impressions or a combination of sense impressions. Even the idea of God, according to Hume, comes from reflecting on our ideas of goodness, power,

David Hume
(1711–1776)

and the like—which we find in ourselves—and "augmenting, without limit, those qualities" (1772/1993, p. 11).

For Hume, reason is essentially powerless when it comes to giving us knowledge about the world. He divided what he calls *objects of human reason* into two kinds: relations of ideas and matters of fact. He placed definitions and mathematics in the category of relations of ideas. These are the only kinds of things about which we can be certain. But, note that this knowledge does not take us very far. We can know that in the English language the word *bachelor* means "unmarried person," but that by itself will not tell us how many bachelors there are, or even whether there are any at all. And, we can know that 5,000 plus 5,000 equals 10,000, but that will not tell us whether there are 10,000 pounds of gold in the world. The second of each of these questions is, for Hume, a matter of fact. According to Hume, reason cannot provide us with any knowledge of matters of fact. He presented the following thought experiment to question Leibniz's claim that it can.

Thought Experiment: Instant Adam

Imagine you are a person with fully formed reason, but without any experience. You might imagine yourself as Adam from the Bible, because according to Genesis, God created him as an adult. Or, you might imagine that you were born in a comatose state but suddenly came out of the coma today. In either case, suppose you are an intelligent adult alive for the first time and you must set out into the world alone. Before long you come to a river that you need to cross. Would you know to hold your breath under water, or would you have to choke first? On the bank of the river is an open fire burning. Would you know to stay a safe distance from it, or would you have to be burned first? Suppose you run into some people and they give you a loaf of bread. Would you know that it was good to eat? What about a tub of mushrooms? Would you know which ones were safe and which were poisonous? Thinking of how children learn things might help you perform this Thought Experiment (From *An Enquiry Concerning Human Understanding*, by David Hume, 1772/1993, p. 17).

Hume thought that Adam would have to learn everything about the world through the trial and error of experience. He challenged those who doubted him to produce a "chain of reasoning" to prove even the most obvious matter of fact: that a rock *must* fall if it is dropped. He was quite confident that no one will succeed in this. We might try saying with Leibniz that the rock must fall because of the force of gravity, but Hume's writing rejects this answer. For an empiricist, all of your ideas have to come from experience, and your experience is limited to seeing unsupported heavy objects falling. You don't ever actually experience an invisible force of gravity.

It is very important to note that Hume did not seriously doubt that there are hidden causes for what happens in the world. He only insisted that because they are hidden, we should not pretend that we understand the real reason why things happen in the manner that they do. And, it is very important to note that Hume did not seriously doubt that the rock will fall when dropped, or that the sun will rise tomorrow. His concern was only to show that our beliefs about the future are not based on reason, and do not constitute knowledge. He called this position *mitigated skepticism*. He doubted that most of our beliefs constitute knowledge, but he does not think that we should, or even could, give up on the beliefs themselves.

So, what is going on when we form beliefs about the future based on past experience if these beliefs are not based on reason? Hume said that they are based on custom or habit. In the past, whenever we have touched snow, for example, it has felt cold. After experiencing this a number of times, we get into the habit of expecting that snow will feel cold. He called this habit of expectation a kind of instinct that is not under our control. Again, we expect the rock to drop because every experience of this kind has been similar. We have, metaphorically speaking, been trained by experience to anticipate that the rock will fall. These habits of expectation, which we regard as knowledge, are really no different in kind from the habit of a dog that instinctively and habitually recoils from a cruel master. Hume concluded:

> And it is certain that we here advance a very intelligible proposition at least, if not a true one, when we assert, that, after the constant conjunction of two objects, heat and flame, for instance, weight and solidity, we are determined by custom alone to expect the one from the appearance of

the other. This hypothesis seems even the only one which explains the difficulty, why we draw, from a thousand instances, an inference, which we are not able to draw from one instance, that is in no respect, different from them. Reason is incapable of any such variation. . . . All inferences from experience, therefore, are effects of custom, not of reasoning. (From *An Enquiry Concerning Human Understanding*, by David Hume, 1772/1993, p. 28.)

Some readers find Hume's skeptical view of human reason rather pessimistic. It seems to reduce us to stimulus-response machines. Can you think of other examples where human beings behave like machines?

Ultimately, the difference between our two authors is religious: Leibniz's rationalism depends on the existence of God and Hume's empiricism doesn't. This is why Leibniz seems more optimistic about human knowledge than Hume. Some philosophers find this optimism attractive. Others, however, would rather not base their views on such a controversial assumption as the existence of God. Do you think rationalism requires the existence of God, or is it possible to be a rationalist without making this assumption? This is an interesting question to consider.

Fallacy Files

Begging the Question

"Begging the question" is another name for circular reasoning. Your opponent commits this fallacy when he uses in his argument the very thing you want him to prove. Suppose you challenge your opponent to provide a good argument for believing in God. He says that you should believe in God because the Bible says that God exists, and that you should believe the Bible because it is the word of God. His proof will work only if you grant that God exists. But, that's exactly what he was supposed to prove! So, he has taken you in a circle of reasoning. The phrase *begging the question* is often misused in common speech to mean "raising the question." This is incorrect, of course, because raising a question is not the same as committing a fallacy.

Reading Comprehension Questions

1. What is rationalism? Which philosopher holds this view?
2. What is empiricism? Which philosopher holds this view?
3. How do we know the world is ordered according to the most logical laws in Leibniz's view?
4. Why does Hume refuse to believe in the *force* of gravity?
5. What is the thought experiment about Adam designed to show? Explain.

Discussion Questions

1. Review the dialogue at the beginning of this chapter. Would Maurice agree more with Leibniz or Hume? What about Jenny? Give evidence.
2. Describe a circumstance under which the sun would not rise tomorrow, or snow would not feel cold, or a rock would not fall.
3. Do you think it is possible to be a rationalist without believing in God? Explain.
4. How do you suppose Hume would account for creativity, believing as he did that all of our ideas come from previous sense experience?

Essay Question

Do you believe that we can have knowledge of the future? Discuss both sides of this debate, making reference to Leibniz and Hume. Then, resolve the debate from your own point of view, presenting an argument in standard form for your conclusion.

Exercises

1. Write a dialogue between Marvin and Alicia. Alicia argues that because we can build machines to associate ideas the way

Hume said that we do, then we are essentially just machines. Marvin argues that there is more to human nature than this.

2. Construct a thought experiment to test Hume's claim that what we call knowledge is merely a set of habits. Remember that habits typically can be broken.

Activities

1. Watch the film *Minority Report*, directed by Stephen Spielberg (2002). What do you think it is trying to say about knowledge of the future?
2. Ask musicians and other artists you know where they get their inspiration.
3. Tape or glue a weight to a beach ball. It will wobble. Watch people's reactions when you first toss or kick it to them. See how long it takes for people to get into the habit of expecting where the wobbling ball will end up.
4. Research Pavlov's dogs and write a report comparing and contrasting Pavlov's conclusions about dogs with Hume's conclusions about human beings.
5. Construct your own example of begging the question.

References

Hume, D. (1993). *An enquiry concerning human understanding.* Indianapolis, IN: Hackett. (Original work published 1772)

Leibniz, G. W. (1951). *Selections* (P. Wiener, Ed.). New York: Charles Scribner's Sons.

Further Reading

Goodman, N. (1983). The new riddle of induction. In N. Goodman (Ed.), *Fact, fiction, and forecast.* (pp. 59–83) Cambridge, MA: Harvard University Press.

Radcliff, E. (2000). *On Hume.* Belmont, CA: Wadsworth.

Reichenbach, H. (1938/2006). *Experience and prediction: An analysis of the foundations of science.* Chicago, IL: University of Chicago Press.

Rescher, N. (1967). *The philosophy of Leibniz.* Upper Saddle River, NJ: Prentice Hall.

Russell, B. (1972). *The problems of philosophy.* New York: Oxford University Press.

Strawson, P. (1952). Dissolving the problem of induction. In P. Strawson (Ed.), *Introduction to logical theory* (pp. 248–263). London: Methuen.

PART 3

The Universe

The Evening Star, 1864,
Jean-Baptiste-Camille
Corot

CHAPTER 9
Is the World Around Us Real?

The Museum

On a class trip to Washington D.C., Miranda and Troy decide to spend their free time together at a museum. As they walk in the door, Miranda slows down and starts looking around her with a puzzled look on her face. Troy suddenly realizes she's fallen behind and turns back toward her.

TROY: This is the right place, Miranda. What's wrong?

MIRANDA: Nothing. It's just that I've got this weird feeling like I've done this before.

TROY: Maybe you've already been here—like when you were little or something.

MIRANDA: No, I've never actually been to this city before.

TROY: Well, you've been to a museum before. All museums look alike.

MIRANDA: No, it's not just this building. It's being here with you, and how I feel, and what I'm wearing, and . . . *<pointing>* that little girl over there in the pink raincoat staring at us. The whole thing—I swear, I've experienced this moment before.

TROY: Oh, I see. *<He looks at her and smiles.>* You're having déjà vu.

MIRANDA: *<Turning toward him, surprised>* What?

TROY: Déjà vu. It's when you feel like you've done something before when you actually haven't. *<He shrugs and turns, ready to continue into the museum.>*

MIRANDA: *<She stays where she is, planting her hands on her hips.>* Troy, hold on. You mean there's a word for it—like it happens all the time?

TROY: *<Turning back, amused>* Yeah, most people get it at some point. I have.

MIRANDA: *<Growing agitated>* Well, what causes it? What does it mean?

TROY: *<Trying to calm her>* It doesn't mean anything, OK? It's just a weird feeling.

MIRANDA: How can you shrug it off like that? It must mean something. *<She looks around, bewildered.>* I know I have experienced all of this before.

TROY: *<Coming toward her>* Miranda, that's impossible.

MIRANDA: No it's not. And, just yesterday I waved to someone I thought was Julie, and it was a complete stranger. Maybe somebody's messing with my senses or my mind. Maybe this whole thing isn't real. It's just some kind of movie, and I've watched it before.

TROY: Well, if this is a movie, it's the most realistic one I've ever seen. *<He reaches over and clasps her arm.>* I don't just see and hear you, I feel you, I smell your perfume. Who could make a movie this real?

MIRANDA: I don't know. *<whispering, clasping his arm>* How about God?

TROY: *<Raising an eyebrow>* Why would God make you watch certain parts of the movie again?

MIRANDA: Maybe I didn't learn what I was supposed to learn the first time.

Questions

- What makes Miranda think the world around her isn't real?
- What makes Troy think it is?
- With whom do you agree more, and why?
- Describe a déjà vu experience you or someone you know had. What do you think caused it?
- Do you think our reality could be like a movie being projected by God? How would you prove that it is or that it isn't?

Is the World Around Us Real?

Have you ever had the feeling that the world as it appears around you is an illusion? This thought may occur to you sometime when your memory deceives you. For example, you're in a hurry to leave home. You set your keys down to put your coat on. You turn back to the counter to grab your keys and they're gone. "I swear I put them right there!" you say to yourself as you begin searching. Five minutes later you find them in your pocket, but you still can't remember putting them there. Or perhaps, you've had the feeling that the world isn't real when your eyes deceive you: "I saw you at the football game last night," you say to a friend. "What do you mean?" she responds, "I didn't go." Or, when your ears deceive you: You hear someone in the other room, but when you go to check it out, nobody's there. "I know I heard something!" you exclaim. Experiences like these, along with déjà vu, seeing mirages, and vivid daydreaming have led some philosophers to question whether our beliefs about the world around us are trustworthy, or even question whether the world is real at all.

Naturally, we all have to *assume* the world is real in order to function on a daily basis. But, a lot of people claim to *know* the world is real. This is a dubious claim. How do you know? If your memory and your senses deceive you some of the time, then they could just as easily deceive you all of the time. It seems there should be some way to distinguish reality from illusion

The American philosopher Wilfrid Sellars (1912–1989) adopted a view known as *scientific realism*. This is the view that while our senses sometimes deceive us, science can give us reliable knowledge about the world. Sellars distinguishes two ways of perceiving reality: the "manifest image" and the "scientific image."

Wilfrid Sellars
(1912–1989)

The manifest image is the world as it seems to us through our five senses, while the scientific image is the world as revealed to us by physics, chemistry, biology, and other sciences.

As an example of these two images, consider your school desk. It should feel solid to you, the top should be smooth, and if it has metal parts they may be cool to the touch. That is the manifest image of the desk. But, science describes a very different desk. Your desk is made of atoms (which you can't see) and between each atom there are vast empty spaces. (So, you are sitting on mostly empty space!) And, the top is not smooth—just look at it through a powerful magnifying glass. So, which is the real desk? Sellars argues that the manifest image is an illusion and the scientific image is true. The scientific image tells us how the world around us really is.

Why should we trust the scientific image? Suppose Benny and Jessica share a carton of orange juice. To Benny, it tastes sweet. To Jessica, it tastes bitter. The reason is that Jessica has just brushed her teeth. If we were to trust the manifest image, we would have to say that the very same orange juice is both sweet and bitter. Sellars points out, however, that the different tastes are an illusion created by the chemical interaction of the juice and the toothpaste. Chemical interactions can be measured objectively in a laboratory. Because laboratory measurements are the same for everyone, we can trust them. The scientific image tells us what's real.

Sellars argues that the manifest image is unreliable because it's a subjective interpretation of the world. This is to say that it exists only in our minds. The following famous thought experiment illustrates the difference between subjective and objective reality.

It may seem strange at first to think that the world isn't exactly how it seems to us. But, it doesn't seem strange when you consider how differently the world seems to other creatures. Flames, for example, consist of molecules in motion. Our eyes see this phenomenon as orange. According to zoologists, however, dogs see the world in black and white. So, flames aren't orange to them. What if human eyes were like dog eyes? Then we never would have had the idea of orange in the first place!

Sellars not only thought that the scientific image is superior to the manifest image, but he thought that we should abandon the manifest image and learn to perceive the world in accordance with the scientific image. He wrote:

> . . . science is making available a more adequate framework
> of entities which *in principle*, at least, could serve all the

Thought Experiment: The Lonely Tree

Suppose you are a great big oak tree in the middle of a forest. During the night last night there was a violent rainstorm. Thunder and lightning crashed all around the hill you grow on. All the little forest animals that live on the hill scampered away into the valley for safety, where they are still hiding. It is dawn. Everything is absolutely still and silent. A number of the trees on the hill have been damaged by the high winds, including you. Rushing water has washed the ground beneath you away and you no longer have a stable foundation. Your branches lean, your roots pull up, your trunk splits, and you crash to the ground. No one was around to hear you fall. Did you make a sound?

It may at first seem obvious that you did. You can imagine the *crreeeeeeeeeeeeeeeek* of the wood splintering, the *whoooooooooooooosh* through the surrounding brush, and the heavy *booooooooom* as you land. You can imagine such sounds because you have heard them before. But, remember: In the story, you are a tree. You have no ears. And, there is no one within hearing distance of your fall. The air vibrates and the ground shakes as you go down. If someone with ears were nearby, these motions would stimulate that person's eardrum. But, if no one with ears is around, then the airwaves will never produce an auditory sensation and hence they will never produce a sound.

What is sound? Is it part of the manifest or the scientific image?

functions, and, in particular, the perceptual functions of the framework we actually employ in everyday life. (From *Science, Perception, and Reality* by Wilfrid Sellars, 1991, p. 97)

He also wrote:

... we (should) *directly* relate the world as conceived by scientific theory to our purposes, and make it *our* world and no longer an alien appendage to the world in which we do our living. We can, of course, as matters now stand, realize this direct incorporation of the scientific image into our way of life only in imagination. But to do so is, if only in imagination, to transcend the dualism of the manifest and scientific images. ... (From *Science, Perception, and Reality* by Wilfrid Sellars, 1991, p. 40)

George Berkeley
(1685–1753)

Of course, to some extent we have already begun to do as Sellars recommends. For example, we now know that the common cold is not really coldness, but rather a bacterial or viral infection.

Even though scientific realism has a lot going for it, the Irish philosopher George Berkeley (1685–1753) pointed out a problem with these beliefs. The scientific realist claims that qualities of the manifest image don't exist objectively outside of the mind because they can appear differently to different observers, and then claims that scientific qualities do exist objectively because they are the same for everyone. On closer examination, however, this seems false. Go back to the example of the desk. Shape is supposed to be one of those objective scientific qualities. And, we can agree that although the desktop feels smooth we can see bumps with a magnifying glass. But, don't stop there. If we used a microscope it would have yet another shape, and an electron microscope would yield yet another. What is the correct scientific image here? Different scientific instruments measure things in different ways and yield different results. Which ones tell us how the world really is?

In Berkeley's view, this question proves that there is really nothing special about the scientific image after all. It too depends on your perspective. So, if the manifest image exists only in the mind, then so does the scientific image. Berkeley came to the radical conclusion that there is no world outside our minds. His view is called *idealism*, because it asserts that only ideas exist.

Does it seem crazy to say that the whole world is nothing but an idea in our minds? Berkeley reasoned that this actually makes more sense than supposing that there are material objects out there. Suppose God created the world and put you in his shoes. He wanted to create some beings like himself, but he knew they would need a world in order to interact with each other. Which would you rather do: Create the world from a lot of messy physical materials or simply project the illusion of physical materials into their minds? For God, projecting the illusion is much simpler. Berkeley asserted that this must be exactly what happened. He wrote:

> To me it is evident, for the reasons you allow of, that sensible things cannot exist otherwise than in a mind or spirit. Whence I conclude, not that they have no real existence, but that, seeing they depend not on my thought, and have an existence distinct from being perceived by me, there must be some other Mind wherein they exist. As sure, therefore, as the sensible world really exists, so sure is there

an infinite omnipresent Spirit who contains and supports it. (From *Three Dialogues Between Hylas and Philonous in Opposition to Sceptics and Atheists* by George Berkeley, 1713/1993, p. 197)

In Berkeley's view, God's mind contains the ideas of everything in the world and he projects these ideas to us in a synchronized way so that the illusion seems like a physical world.

Many philosophers have tried to save scientific realism from idealist criticisms. Others have simply conceded that Berkeley is right: There is something wrong with the notion of objective reality. Although regarding the world as an illusion is not very common in Western culture, it is a standard belief among Buddhists. Richard Gere and Keanu Reeves, two Hollywood actors who converted to Buddhism, agree with Berkeley that the material world does not exist.

Would it change your life any if one day you found out for sure that the world is an illusion? Perhaps not. Because all of the same things you are used to seeing and doing would continue to be part of the illusion, it may not make much difference in how you live your life. So, what is the point in wondering about it one way or the other? The point is to realize that you don't really know as much as you thought you did. The great Supreme Court justice Oliver Wendell Holmes once said that doubting one's first principles is the mark of the civilized person. This is a surprising claim. It seems as though a perfectly civilized person would be certain of everything. But, it turns out that the reverse is true: Knowing what you don't know is sometimes even more important than knowing what you know!

Fallacy Files

Ad Ignorantiam

In a court of law an individual is innocent until proven guilty. Do you think this principle applies to beliefs? In particular, are you entitled to consider realism true until it is proven false? Perhaps. But, notice that Berkeley could use this same reasoning concerning idealism. After all, no one can prove that God is not projecting the world to us as an illusion. To philosophers, beliefs cannot be considered innocent in the same way people are. Assuming something is true just because it hasn't been proven false (or vice versa) is a fallacious form of argumentation called *ad ignorantiam* (meaning "from ignorance"). Ad ignorantiam is a mistake because it is a way of avoiding the burden of proof. You should look for positive reasons for your beliefs rather than just holding them by default.

Reading Comprehension Questions

1. What is scientific realism? Which philosopher holds this view?
2. What is idealism? Which philosopher holds this view?
3. What is the difference between the manifest image and the scientific image, according to Sellars?
4. Why does Berkeley think that the scientific image is just as subjective as the manifest image?
5. What is the thought experiment about the lonely tree designed to show? Explain.

Discussion Questions

1. Review the dialogue at the beginning of this chapter. Would Miranda agree more with Sellars or Berkeley? What about Troy? Give evidence.
2. Describe a time when your senses deceived you. Do you still trust them? Why or why not?
3. Identify an object in the room and say how it would be described by both the manifest and scientific images. Do you think Berkeley is correct to suppose that there is really no difference between the two? Explain.
4. According to Berkeley, to say the world is an illusion is not the same as saying that we are imagining it. Explain the difference.

Essay Question

Do you believe the world around you is real? Discuss both sides of this debate, making reference to Sellars and Berkeley. Then, resolve the debate from your own point of view, presenting an argument in standard form for your conclusion.

Exercises

1. Write a dialogue between Kelly and Gordon. Kelly argues that her new dress is really green. Gordon argues that it isn't really any color.
2. Construct a thought experiment to test the claim that human eyes see things as they really are.

Activities

1. Watch the movie *The Matrix*, directed by the Wachowski brothers (1999). How is the world an illusion in this story?
2. Write a letter to a friend in which you try to convince them that the world is an illusion.
3. Design an illusionary world.
4. Make a list of all the strange things about your life that make you wonder whether this world might be an illusion.
5. Research Buddhism and write a report on why Buddhists believe the world is an illusion.

References

Berkeley, G. (1993). *Three dialogues between Hylas and Philonous in opposition to sceptics and atheists.* In *The Harvard Classics* (Vol. 37, pt. 2; pp. 197). New York: P.F. Collier & Son. (Original work published 1713)

Sellars, W. (1991). *Science, perception, and reality.* Atascadero, CA: Ridgeview Publishing.

Further Reading

Austin, J. L. (1962). The argument from illusion. In G. J. Warnock (Ed.), *Sense and sensibilia* (pp. 1–77). New York: Oxford University Press.

Ayer, A. J. (1958). The argument from illusion. In A. J. Ayer (Ed.), *The foundations of empirical knowledge* (pp. 1–57). New York: St. Martin's Press.

Bennett, J. (2001). *Learning from six philosophers* (Vol. 2). New York: Oxford University Press.

Blackburn, S. (1999). *Think: A compelling introduction to philosophy.* Oxford, England: Oxford University Press.

Churchland, P. (1986). *Scientific realism and the plasticity of mind.* New York: Cambridge University Press.

Locke, J. (1995). *An essay concerning human understanding.* Retrieved April 27, 2007, from http://www.ilt.columbia.edu/publications/Projects/digitexts/locke/understanding/chapter0208.html (Original work published 1689)

Neta, R. (2003). Contextualism and the problem of the external world. *Philosophy and Phenomenological Research, 66,* 1–21.

Popkin, R. H., & Stroll, A. (2001). *Skeptical philosophy for everyone.* Amherst, NY: Prometheus.

Russell, B. (1914). *Our knowledge of the external world.* Chicago, IL: Open Court.

White, D. A. (2000). Gifted students and philosophy: The sound of a tree falling in the forest. *Gifted Child Today, 23*(4), 28–33.

CHAPTER 10
Does the Universe Have a Beginning?

The Attic

After his grandmother dies, Corey is asked to sort through her attic. He invites his friend Danielle over to help. They've been packing strange and interesting objects into boxes for a few hours and are nearly finished. Pushing through some broken furniture into a dark corner, Corey calls Danielle over.

COREY: Check this out! *<Clearing off a small table with a machine on it>* It's an old record player. *<Examining it>* It doesn't even plug in. You have to crank it to make it play. *<He cranks it and a little warped music tinkles out.>*

DANIELLE: That's a record player? It must be older than God.

COREY: It's old alright. *<He scowls and stops cranking.>* But, not older than God.

DANIELLE: *<She crosses her arms on her chest.>* That's just an expression, Corey.

COREY: I know. I'm just saying it doesn't make any sense. Nothing's older than God.

DANIELLE: How do you know? *<She sits down on an old couch.>*

COREY: Danielle, if God exists, then he made everything, so nothing could have existed before him. *<He wipes his hands on his jeans and walks over to the couch.>*

DANIELLE: God can't have made everything. *<She picks up a rubber ball and tosses it between hands.>* The law of the conservation of energy says matter can't be created or destroyed. So, matter has been around forever. God just shaped it into stars and planets.

COREY: *<Shaking his head>* That law only started to be a law at the moment of creation. Before then, there wasn't anything—no stars, no planets, and no scientific laws. Just God.

DANIELLE: I don't see it that way at all, Corey. What would God be doing all by himself like that? Sure, he created *our* universe at some point. But, there were other universes before that. I think for as long as he's existed he's been forming and reforming matter.

COREY: But, God's existed forever, Danielle. There never was a time before God.

DANIELLE: Well, then matter and God are equally old. *<She tosses the ball to him.>*

COREY: Danielle, haven't you ever heard of the Big Bang? It's scientifically proven that our universe started billions of years ago in a gigantic explosion.

DANIELLE: I know. But, nobody knows what happened before the Big Bang. I think our big bang was set off by a prior universe collapsing in on itself until it had to explode. Universes have been collapsing and exploding like that forever. Ours is just the latest.

COREY: *<He sits down on the couch and tosses the ball to her.>* Well, I guess that's possible. But, I'd rather believe our universe is the only one—that God made it special.

DANIELLE: I hate to tell you, hon, but what you want has got nothing to do with it.

Questions

- What makes Danielle think that a universe has always existed in some form?
- Why does Corey disagree?
- With whom do you agree more, and why?
- If there is a God, do you think he has existed for an infinite amount of time? Why or why not?
- If you were God would you make just one universe or would you make an infinite succession of universes? Explain.

Does the Universe Have a Beginning?

Here's a tough question for you: How old is God? If God exists, he must be very, very old. Most people conceive of God as being without beginning and without end. If this conception is correct, then the answer to our question is that God is infinitely old. He doesn't have a beginning like the rest of us. He just always was.

It's hard to conceive of something without a beginning, because every individual object that exists in the universe has one. But, what about the universe as a whole? Could it be infinitely old?

Astrophysicists have traced the history of the universe back to a cosmic explosion, called the Big Bang, which occurred billions of years ago. But, was there anything before the Big Bang? Although it has been established beyond any reasonable doubt that the Big Bang happened, no one knows for sure whether it really was the beginning.

In fact, recent research indicates that our Big Bang may just have been the latest in a long series of cosmic explosions. Some think the series may be infinite just like a set of integers: Whether you are looking forward or looking backward, you can keep going forever. Although astrophysicists have been discussing the idea of an infinitely old universe much more in recent years, the idea is not new. The ancient Greek philosopher Aristotle (384–322 BC) vigorously defended this view.

Aristotle argued that it is impossible for the universe to have a beginning. To prove this, he tackled the question: What is time? Today, when we define time we think of clocks. As the hands of the clock go around and around they measure time going by. Liv-

Aristotle
(384–322 BC)

Thought Experiment: The Big Sleep

If there is a God and he created the universe out of nothing at some time in the past, what was he doing before that? Try to imagine what it would be like to be God at the moment of creation. Notice that you have been alone for a very long time. In fact, you've been all by yourself for an infinite amount of time already! Suppose the set of integers represents time and zero designates the moment of creation. There are an infinite number of negative integers before zero. If you were happy to spend an infinite amount of time by yourself, what suddenly changed your mind? Some philosophers believe this thought experiment shows there really is no God and the universe has always existed. Others think it shows God is beyond all temporal measure, that his existence is somehow timeless. Still others think that this shows that our limited minds are not up to the task of really and fully understanding such concepts as "God" and "infinity." What do you think it shows?

ing before the invention of clocks, Aristotle thought of the sun going around and around the earth. Regardless of how you define time, you must measure it through some kind of constant motion. This is because time is a change from the past into the future. The present moment, *now*, is just a dividing line between what was and what will be.

Aristotle reasoned that it is impossible for the universe to have a beginning because it is impossible for there to be a first moment. He wrote:

> Now since time cannot exist and is unthinkable apart from the moment, and the moment a kind of middle-point,

uniting as it does in itself both a beginning and an end, a beginning of future time and an end of past time, it follows that there must always be time: for the extremity of the last period of time that we take must be found in some moment, since time contains no point of contact for us except the moment. Therefore, since the moment is both a beginning and an end, there must always be time on both sides of it. (From *Physics*, by Aristotle, 350 BC, [http://classics.mit.edu/Aristotle/physics.8.vii.html])

How could there be a first *now*? Because every *now* is a dividing line between past and future, even the first now would have to have a past. But, every past was once *now*. So our first *now* would not have been the first after all! Because there cannot be a first *now*, time must have existed forever.

In the end, according to Aristotle, the universe is nothing but a very large quantity of matter in motion: revolving planets, pulsating stars, and swirling galaxies. Nowhere does the universe stay still. Think of the quietest place on earth, such as your grandmother's attic. Even though it may seem motionless, it is cruising around the sun at speed of about 67,000 miles per hour. Because time is measured by matter in motion, and time has existed forever, matter must have been in motion forever too. Aristotle's view is called *cyclicism*, because it holds that the universe goes around and around through endless cycles, the constant companion of time.

The medieval philosopher Thomas Aquinas (1225–1274) considered himself an Aristotelian in most respects. Cyclicism, however, is one aspect of Aristotle's philosophy he rejected. Aquinas famously presented five proofs of the existence of God. In the first one, he argued that there must be a God because there must have been someone to start the universe. This argument hinges on the idea that the universe could not have existed forever. Aquinas wrote:

Thomas Aquinas
(1225–1274)

> It is certain, and evident to our senses, that in the world some things are in motion. Now whatever is in motion is put in motion by another. . . . If that by which it is put in motion be itself put in motion, then this also must needs be put in motion by another, and that by another again. But this cannot go on to infinity, because then there would be no first mover, and, consequently, no other mover; see-

ing that subsequent movers move only inasmuch as they are put in motion by the first mover; as the staff moves only because it is put in motion by the hand. Therefore it is necessary to arrive at a first mover, put in motion by no other; and this everyone understands to be God. (From *The Summa Theologica*, by Thomas Aquinas, 1274, [http://newadvent.org/summa/100203.html])

Aquinas pictured the universe like a set of dominoes; someone has to set off the chain reaction. If not, the universe never would have started moving in the first place.

The domino effect is the way things usually work in the world around us. Consider how news spreads. You tell your friend you've fallen in love. She tells her neighbors. They tell their babysitter. She tells her cousin. And, he tells Oprah Winfrey. Now, Oprah never would have gotten the news if you hadn't started the chain by telling your friend. Can you think of other examples of the domino effect? Aquinas figured the universe works the same way.

Aquinas's view is called *creation ex nihilo*, because it holds that the universe was created out of nothing (*ex nihilo* means "out of nothing" in Latin). Creation *ex nihilo* is the view opposing cyclicism because it asserts that, even if the universe has been cycling around and around for a long time there had to be a first cycle. Aquinas lived before the discovery of the big bang, but if he were alive today he might identify it as the moment of creation.

Aquinas's view was intuitive in so far as everything we see around us has a beginning. This seems to imply that the universe itself should have a beginning too. On the other hand, Aquinas's view was that the universe began from nothing and this is *unlike* anything we see around us. Consider a candy bar. It has a beginning, but not from nothing. It came from ingredients in a factory. And, the ingredients came from crops on farms and other chemical factories. And, the crops on farms came from the rain and the dirt. And, even the rain and the dirt came from something, and so on, and so on, without end. Likewise for everything else we know of, including human beings. So, Aquinas' creation *ex nihilo* view is not as obvious as it seems. It's claiming that something can come from nothing, but we have never witnessed such a thing. In contrast to Aquinas, Aristotle insists that it is a law of nature that nothing can come from nothing. This is why Aristotle held firmly to cyclicism.

Many people think that the question of whether the universe had a beginning makes a big difference for human beings. In their view, if the universe has always existed, then there is no need to believe in God. They think cyclicism implies that human beings evolved by accident during the last cycle and so our lives are ultimately meaningless. Although it is possible to draw this conclusion, it's interesting to note that Aristotle himself did not see life as meaningless at all. He even believed in a kind of God or eternal spirit who has coexisted forever with the world. There are a lot more possibilities than you might think.

Fallacy Files

Irrelevant Authority

People often refer to authorities to support their arguments. For example, when trying to prove that the universe is not infinitely old, someone might point out that the Bible says, "In the beginning God created the heavens and the Earth." Would this information be relevant in deciding for yourself what to believe? Philosophers don't think so. Appealing to an irrelevant authority is a fallacious form of reasoning. Look on the Internet and you'll find an "authority" swearing to any number of false claims. For example, you might see an online ad claim "Dr. Smedley Jones M.D. attests that the new Wonderthin diet pill will make you lose 10 pounds overnight!" Because it's hard to know which authorities to trust, philosophers turn to reason and evidence to support their arguments instead.

Reading Comprehension Questions

1. What is cyclicism? Which philosopher holds this view?
2. What is creation *ex nihilo*? Which philosopher holds this view?
3. Why can there be no first *now*, according to Aristotle?
4. Why does there have to be a God, according to Aquinas?
5. What do philosophers think the thought experiment about God's big sleep shows? Explain.

Discussion Questions

1. Review the dialogue at the beginning of this chapter. Would Corey agree more with Aristotle or with Aquinas? What about Danielle? Give evidence.

2. It is a principle of physics that matter is energy and energy can never be created or destroyed. Does this show that the universe has always been or that the principles of physics do not always hold?
3. Imagine that everything in the universe suddenly freezes motionless. Would time continue to go by? How could you tell?
4. Some people think the universe could have started from nothing all by itself. Do you agree? Why or why not?

Essay Question

Do you believe the universe had a beginning? Discuss both sides of this debate, making reference to Aristotle and Aquinas. Then, resolve the debate from your own point of view, presenting an argument in standard form for your conclusion.

Exercises

1. Write a dialogue between Amir and Desirae. Amir argues that God's existence is timeless. Desirae argues that it isn't.
2. Construct a thought experiment to test the claim that it is impossible for anything around us to come from nothing.

Activities

1. Watch the movie, *The Big Bang*, directed by James Toback (1990). Do you think it shows how the history of the universe is relevant to the meaning of life?
2. Draw the set of integers on a number line showing the difference between cyclicism and creation *ex nihilo*.
3. Write a report on current scientific research concerning what caused the Big Bang.
4. Interview family and friends. Do they think it is possible that the universe has always existed? What would it mean to them if it did?

5. Watch the PBS series *The Elegant Universe* (found online at http://www.pbs.org/wgbh/nova/elegant/program.html) and write a report on how string theory is relevant to the beginning of the universe.

References

Aristotle. (n.d.) *Physics* (Book VIII; R. P. Hardie & R. K. Gaye, Trans.). Retrieved April 30, 2007, from http://classics.mit.edu/Aristotle/physics.8.viii.html (Original work published 350 BC)

St. Thomas Aquinas. (1920). *The summa theologica* (First Part, Question 2, Article 3; Fathers of the English Dominican Province, Trans.). Retrieved April 30, 2007, from http://www.newadvent.org/summa/100203.htm (Original work published 1274.)

Further Reading

Albright, J. R. (2000). Cosmology: What one needs to know. *Zygon, 35,* 173–180.

Hawking, S. (1988). *A brief history of time: From the big bang to black holes.* New York: Bantam Books.

Morriston, W. (2003). Must metaphysical time have a beginning? *Faith and Philosophy, 20*(3), 288–306.

Oderberg, D. S. (2003). The beginning of existence. *International Philosophical Quarterly, 43*(2), 145–157.

Oppy, G. (2001). Time, successive addition, and the cosmological arguments. *Philosophia-Christi, 3,* 181–191.

Smith, Q. (2002). Time was created by a timeless point: An atheist explanation of spacetime. In G. B. Ganssle & D. M. Woodruff, *God and time* (pp. 112–113.) Oxford, England: Oxford University Press.

Svitil, K. A. (2003). Cosmologists play Chicken Little. *Discover, 24,* 12.

Veneziano, G. (2004, May). The myth of the beginning of time. *Scientific American,* 54–64.

CHAPTER 11
Is the Universe Finite or Infinite in Size?

The Ocean

Maria and Tom are walking barefoot on the beach at the Atlantic Ocean. As the sun sets, a light breeze begins to blow. Waves roll rhythmically onto the shore. Seagulls swoop past and call softly. Maria picks up a flat stone and skips it as far as she can across the water.

MARIA: Just think how big the ocean is! I could stand here looking at it all night. *<She moves closer to Tom.>* It seems like it goes on forever.

TOM: *<Smiling at her>* It seems like it goes on forever because the curvature of the Earth prevents us from seeing the other side. But trust me, the other side is there.

MARIA: *<She winces.>* Why do you have to get so scientific all the time? Can't you be a bit romantic sometimes?

TOM: *<Approaching and putting his arm around her.>* I brought you here didn't I? *<He points to the sky.>* And, look, the stars are coming out. If you think the ocean is big, just think how big the sky is.

MARIA: *<She follows his gaze.>* Yeah, I know. It may be true that the ocean has another side, but the sky really does go on forever.

TOM: *<He turns to look at her.>* I hate to say this, Maria, but I don't agree.

MARIA: <*She pulls away, putting her hands on her hips.*> What—you think if you go far enough in space you eventually come to the other side? What is it, a wall or something? Yeah right. A wall with a sign on it: "You are now leaving space. Come back for a visit again soon." <*She laughs.*>

TOM: Well, no, not a wall, silly. <*He starts walking again.*> It's just that it can't go on forever because scientists have measured how far away the furthest stars are.

MARIA: But Tom, the stars are getting further and further apart all the time because the universe is expanding. Everything started with the Big Bang. It was like an explosion spewing matter outward in an ever-growing sphere. Because there is not enough gravity in space to stop the matter from moving outward, the sphere will keep growing forever.

TOM: That sphere you're talking about is the sum total of space. It may keep growing, but at any given point it is a finite size. It's just like this: Someone could start with one and keep counting forever, but no matter how long they count, any number they actually say will be a finite number.

MARIA: I see what you mean, but you're wrong about one thing. You say the growing sphere is space itself but it isn't. The growing sphere is the universe and "space" is the space it is growing into. Space has to be infinite in order to contain an infinite expansion.

TOM: <*Sighs*> So much for romance. I think this is going to be a long night.

Questions

- Why does Tom think that space is finite in size?
- Why does Maria think it has to be infinite?
- With whom do you agree more, and why?
- Do you think it is possible for something to keep expanding forever? How do you know?
- Is space the same as nothingness? Is nothingness something? Explain.

How Big is the Universe?

Stephen Hawking
(1942–)

The question of whether space is finite or infinite in size is very difficult to think about. Is there any point to trying? According to the English scientist Stephen Hawking (1942–) there is. In his view, thinking about this question helps us figure out whether God exists, and if so, what God is like. Furthermore, wondering about infinity is a kind of mental exercise that makes us better thinkers. Even if we conclude that we can't answer the question, we still have learned something important, especially if we figure out why we can't answer the question. Do you agree?

Human beings have been wondering about the size of the universe for a very long time. In his poem *On the Nature of Things*, the ancient Roman thinker Lucretius (c. 95–52 BC) presents a thought experiment like the following to show that space must be infinite in size.

Thought Experiment: Lucretius' Spear

Suppose you rocket to the furthest reaches of outer space and hurl a spear. Do you think it would it fly on and on forever or do you think something would eventually stop and block it? Lucretius thinks it would fly on and on forever. He argues as follows: Either the spear continues or it bounces off some sort of wall. But, if there is a wall, then there must be something on the other side of the wall, and what could there be but more space?

Although this answer seems reasonable, there may be another way to explain the spear's continued flight. If you stand on the surface of the moon and hurl a spear, it will fly on and on forever because there is not enough gravity to pull it down. Even though it looks like it's moving in a straight line, it's actually curving in a giant circle around the moon. If space itself is a giant sphere, this could explain the spear's continued flight.

Albert Einstein
(1879–1955)

So, is the universe finite or infinite in size? The 20th century scientist, Albert Einstein (1879–1955) argues that *physics*, the study of nature, furnishes an answer. In his view, people find thinking about this question difficult because they are using their imaginations instead of numerical formulas. He wrote:

All these space-like concepts already belong to pre-scientific thought, along with concepts like pain, goal, purpose, etc. from the field of psychology. . . . The physicist seeks to reduce colours and tones to vibrations, the physiologist thought and pain to nerve processes, in such a way that the psychical element as such is eliminated from the causal nexus of existence. . . . Science has taken over from pre-scientific thought the concepts of space, time, and material object, and has modified them and rendered them more precise. (From *Relativity: The Special and General Theory*, by Albert Einstein, 1920/1961, p. 141–2)

According to Einstein, science renders the concept of space more precise by describing it mathematically. In mathematical terms, the universe can be finite in size while at the same time be infinite in the sense of being "unbounded."

The best way to understand Einstein's concept of space is to think of a vacuum. A vacuum is a completely empty container. All the air is pumped out so that there is absolutely nothing filling the space. Imagine inserting a balloon into the mouth of a large vacuum without breaking the seal. As you blow up the balloon it expands into nothing. Air is inside the balloon but there is literally nothing on the outside of the balloon. So, the balloon is finite, because it is a measurable size, but at the same time it is unbounded because nothing limits its expansion. It's easy enough to picture this as long as there is a container to hold the nothingness. When it comes to outer space, however, there is no container. The universe is space expanding into infinite nothingness, according to Einstein. He grants that it is impossible for the human psyche to imagine this, insisting that we can bypass the psyche and demonstrate it mathematically.

According to the German philosopher Immanuel Kant (1724–1804), however, we can never eliminate the role that the human psyche plays in demonstration. In his view, our picture of the world is a composite of two things. First, there is the reality that exists out there by itself. Kant calls this the *matter of experience*. Second, there are the ideas supplied by our own minds. He calls these the *form of experience*. His theory is that human beings cannot know how reality is by itself because our minds are always filtering the raw data we receive through our ideas.

An analogy may help to clarify Kant's point. Imagine that you suffered a rare eye disease as a baby. In order to cure you, doc-

Immanuel Kant
(1724–1804)

tors had to install permanent tinted contact lenses on your eyes. You know about this, because you can see them in the mirror, and your parents told you about your eye disease. So, you know that your perception of the world is different from that of other people, and that it is a composite of what is out there and how the lenses filter the image of what is out there. But, because you can never remove the lenses, you can never know what the world looks like in itself. In the same way, Kant holds that although human beings can know things about our composite world, we can never have any knowledge of reality itself.

Kant's account of perception is one type of *metaphysics* (which literally means "beyond the study of nature"), because it hypothesizes a reality that transcends what we perceive. Nevertheless, he denies that we can have any metaphysical *knowledge*. In his view, metaphysics shows that some questions have no answer. The question about the size of the universe is like this. He wrote:

> When I speak of objects in time and in space, it is not of things in themselves, of which I know nothing, but of things in appearance, that is, of experience, as the particular way of cognizing objects which is afforded to man. I must not say of what I think in time or in space, that in itself, and independent of these my thoughts, it exists in space and in time; for in that case I should contradict myself; because space and time, together with the appearances in them, are nothing existing in themselves and outside of my representations, but are themselves only modes of representation, and it is palpably contradictory to say, that a mere mode of representation exists without our representation. Objects of the senses therefore exist only in experience; whereas to give them a self-subsisting existence apart from experience or before it, is merely to represent to ourselves that experience actually exists apart from experience or prior to it.
>
> Now if I inquire after the magnitude of the world, as to space and time, it is equally impossible, as regards all my notions, to declare it infinite or to declare it finite. For neither assertion can be contained in experience, because experience either of an infinite space, or of an infinite time elapsed, or again, of the boundary of the world by a void space, or by an antecedent void time, is impossible; these are mere ideas. This quantity of the world, which is deter-

mined in either way, should therefore exist in the world itself apart from all experience. This contradicts the notion of a world of sense, which is merely a complex of the appearances whose existence and connection occur only in our representations, that is, in experience, since this latter is not an object in itself, but a mere mode of representation. Hence it follows, that as the concept of an absolutely existing world of sense is self-contradictory, the solution of the problem concerning its quantity, whether attempted affirmatively or negatively, is always false. (From *Prolegomena to Any Future Metaphysics, Part III* by Immanuel Kant, 1783/1989, pp. 108–109)

Perhaps other creatures, such as aliens or angels, who perceive the world in a different way, could experience the magnitude of the world and answer the question once and for all. But, as human beings, we are wise to recognize our own limitations.

What makes Einstein's "finite but unbounded" theory appealing is that its mathematical models allow us to make very accurate predictions. In presenting this theory, Einstein insists that math captures the structure of reality better than our imagination can. Perhaps people like Einstein, who can think in purely mathematical terms, can escape the limitations Kant identifies. Or perhaps, mathematics is just another kind of imagination. As always, it is up to you to decide.

Fallacy Files

False Dilemma

A false dilemma occurs when you are offered a choice between two options with the implication that there are no further options. For example, if it's raining out, your mother might say "take your umbrella or you will get wet," but you can avoid this false dilemma by not going out at all. As another example from this chapter, Lucretius assumes that the question at hand is whether the universe is finite or infinite. But, Einstein shows how it may be both and Kant shows how it may be neither. You do not always have to choose. Philosophers often tackle a difficult problem by showing that there is a completely new way of thinking about it.

Reading Comprehension Questions

1. What is physics? Which philosopher represents this discipline?
2. What is metaphysics? Which philosopher represents this discipline?
3. How does science render the concept of space more precise, according to Einstein?
4. Why can't we know how big the universe is, according to Kant?
5. What does Lucretius think the thought experiment about the spear shows? Explain.

Discussion Questions

1. Review the dialogue at the beginning of this chapter. Would Maria agree more with Einstein or Kant? What about Tom? Give evidence.
2. Try to think of something (other than the universe) that can be described in purely mathematical terms but not pictured in the imagination.
3. Do you agree with Stephen Hawking that it is useful to explore big questions even if you can't answer them for certain? Why or why not?

Essay Question

Do you believe that we can know the size of the universe? Discuss both sides of this debate, making reference to Einstein and Kant. Then, resolve the debate from your own point of view, presenting an argument in standard form for your conclusion.

Exercises

1. Write a dialogue between Katie and John. Katie argues that math is just another form of imagination. John argues that it isn't.
2. Construct a thought experiment to test the claim that the human mind is limited.

Activities

1. Watch the movie *Time Bandits*, directed by Terry Gilliam (1991). Do the portraits of space and time in this film resemble those of any of the thinkers discussed in this chapter?
2. Look at Salvador Dali's painting "Crucifixion." What does it say about your perception of reality?
3. Read Robert Heinlein's story "And He Built a Crooked House" and Arthur C. Clark's story "Technical Error," both of which explore alternative ways of thinking about space.
4. Explore the work of Dutch artist M. C. Escher. What might his optical illusions tell you about our spatial perceptions?
5. Research current cosmological theories and write a report comparing and contrasting them.

References

Einstein, A. (1961). *Relativity: The special and general theory*. New York: Crown Publishers. (Original work published 1920)

Hawking, S. (1988). *A brief history of time: From the big bang to black holes.* New York: Bantam Books.

Kant, I. (1783/1989) *Prolegomena to any future metaphysics* (P. Carus, Trans.). LaSalle, IL: Open Court.

Lucretius. (1977). *De rerum natura*. New York: W. W. Norton. (Original work published before 50 B.C.)

Further Reading

Abbott, E. (1952). *Flatland.* New York: Dover.

Boslough, J. (1985). *Stephen Hawking's universe.* New York: William Morrow.

Einstein, A. (1984). *The meaning of relativity.* Princeton, NJ: Princeton University Press. (Original work published 1921)

Strawson, P. (1966). *The bounds of sense.* London: Methuen & Co.

Thomson, G. (2000). *On Kant.* Belmont, CA: Wadsworth.

CHAPTER 12
What Is the Difference Between Genuine Science and Pseudoscience?

The Festival Booths

Cameron and Tonya are at a summer street festival. One of the booths advertises that you can get a complete astrological chart—a personality analysis and predictions about your future—for only $25. At the booth next door, a woman claims to be able to do the same thing by reading palms.

TONYA: I want to get a reading about my future, but I can't decide whether to go for an astrology or palm reading. What do you think?

CAMERON: <In an outraged tone.>What do I think? I'll give you a prediction for free. These things are all frauds, and I predict that you will be $25 poorer and won't learn a thing you didn't already know. Things like astrology are called "pseudoscience," meaning fake science, because they make things up in order to take your money.

TONYA: If they're so fake, Smartie Pants, then why are people lining up?

CAMERON: <He looks around and thinks for a minute.> I don't know for sure. I think it may be wishful thinking: People just really want to believe it's true. At any rate, people talk it up. If you've just spent that much money you're going to work real hard to make what they say fit you. Otherwise, you'll feel like a total dupe.

TONYA: OK, but my mom visits this booth every year, and she says that their predictions are accurate. How do you explain so many people consulting seers again and again?

CAMERON: <*Smacking her shoulder*> Because they're sheep who want to be told what to do instead of thinking for themselves!

TONYA: <*Sharply*> Don't be mean. Just last week my horoscope said I would have trouble with relationships, and the next day you and I had a fight.

CAMERON: Did your horoscope predict trouble today?

TONYA: <*Puzzled.*> No.

CAMERON: We're having a fight now, aren't we? Why wasn't that predicted?

TONYA: They can't predict everything. . . .

CAMERON: Look, these predictions are so vague that they can apply to almost every person and situation. <*He picks up some discarded astrology readings.*> Look at these: "You will find romance where you least expect it." "Changes at work will bring financial opportunities." And, here's the one you had: "You will experience trouble in your personal relationships."

TONYA: Well, at least I'm not the only one dealing with a lug like you.

Questions

- Why does Tonya think astrology works?
- Why does Cameron think it is a fraud?
- With whom do you agree more, and why?
- Have you ever had your fortune told? If so, was it accurate? If not, would you ever want to?
- If a friend of yours announced a major life decision (for example, dropping out of school or ending a relationship) based on a visit to an astrology booth, what would be your reaction? Explain.

Science Vs. Pseudoscience

Do you believe astrologists and fortunetellers can predict your future by knowing your date of birth and looking at the palm of your hand? Most people who read horoscopes read them for amusement and not for instructions on what to do. But, if you think that there might be some truth to astrology, try this experiment. Have a friend read your horoscope to you for 10 days. Five of the days should be the horoscope for your sign while the other five should be the horoscope for another sign, but you will not know which is which. Keep a daily record of how accurate the horoscope is and see whether you can tell which days you had the right horoscope and which days you had the wrong one. If astrology is true, you should be able to tell the difference. If you can't tell the difference, then there is no reason to believe in it.

The world is a mixed-up tangle of scientific facts and fraudulent fictions, and it is not always easy to tell which is which. We are constantly bombarded by seemingly scientific claims about products you can buy—"Wonderthin diet pills will make you lose 10 pounds overnight!" "Vitalix energy drink will prevent cancer and cure the common cold!" Fraudulent products not only waste your money, they can be harmful to your health, particularly if you neglect proper medical treatment as a result of consuming such products. We all need to be able to make informed judgments about such claims. This is to say we need to be able to distinguish science from pseudoscience (or fake science).

What makes a claim scientific is its ability to explain a given phenomenon and make predictions about it. A scientific theory is a set of claims that meet these goals by appealing to laws of nature or general principles. But, there is controversy over what makes such a theory worthy of belief.

Many philosophers insist that a theory is worthy of belief if we can confirm it by experience or experiment. This is called *verification*. For example, the claim that sodium and chlorine combine in a 1 to 1 ratio to make table salt is worthy of belief because it has been verified many times. Claims that have not been verified are still considered scientific if we at least know how to verify them. For example, the claim that there is an underground supply of water on the planet Mars is verifiable even though we have not yet verified it. In contrast, suppose Ted says he believes "that there are seven angels in the first circle of heaven." This is not a scientific claim, because there is no way to verify it.

Sir Isaac Newton
(1643–1747)

Sir Isaac Newton (1643–1747), the English scientist known for discovering the laws of gravity, defended verification. He wrote:

I frame no hypotheses; for whatever is not deduced from the phenomena is to be called an hypothesis; and hypotheses, whether metaphysical or physical, whether of occult qualities or mechanical, have no place in experimental philosophy. In this philosophy particular propositions are inferred from the phenomena . . . and to us it is enough that gravity does really exist, and act according to the laws which we have explained, and abundantly serves to account for all the motions of the celestial bodies, and of our sea. (From *Philosophiae Naturalis Principia Mathematica,* by Sir Isaac Newton, 1687/1962, p. 547)

According to Newton, good scientists restrict their theorizing to what can be directly verified by experience. The advantage of this approach is that, once a theory is confirmed, it can be accepted as the truth.

Although verification promises to provide certainty, some philosophers reject it as unreliable. Consider the following example. Jill claims that wearing a rabbit's foot helps her run faster at track meets. She wears the rabbit's foot at every meet and has a great season. She insists that her experience verifies her claim. But, she also wore pink underwear to each of those track meets. So, there is no more reason to attribute her success to the rabbit's foot than to the pink underwear. Jill believes that the rabbit's foot has a special power and the pink underwear doesn't, but this belief is unjustified because both are equally confirmed.

Sir Karl Popper
(1902–1994)

The Austrian philosopher of science Sir Karl Popper (1902–1994) presents another way to judge whether a theory is worthy of belief. According to Popper, we should not only try to show that our theories fit known facts, we should try to show that they don't. This is called *falsification.* It may seem a bit odd to try to prove something false when you believe it to be true. But, Popper's point is that, by trying to prove that a theory is false, we put it through a test. If the theory passes the test, then we can continue to believe in it; if it fails, then we are better off with a newer and better theory anyway. We should become more confident in a theory, not when we find confirming instances for it, but when it survives falsification.

In the middle of the 19th century, for example, some people began to question Sir Isaac Newton's physics. So, an astronomer made a prediction based on Newton's physics. He said that if Newton's theory of physics is correct then there must be an undiscovered planet in a certain region of the sky. Years later, when a strong enough telescope was finally built, astronomers examined this region of the sky and, sure enough, they discovered a planet, today known as Neptune. This prediction was a test for Newton's theory. If they had not found any planet where Newton's physics said it should be, then his theory would have been falsified.

Popper does not hold, however, that passing one test proves a theory true. Just like passing one calculus test does not turn you into a mathematician, making one successful, but risky (meaning that you don't know in advance how it will turn out), prediction does not turn a theory into an accepted truth. In order for a theory to become an accepted truth, it would have to pass all of the tests. But, this is probably impossible because we can always think of new tests.

Newtonians learned this the hard way. Although Newton's theory passed one test by predicting the discovery of Neptune, it failed another test later. In the 20th century, Albert Einstein developed a new theory of physics that contradicted Newton's theory. To decide between them, scientists designed a test that would falsify one of them and so increase our confidence in the other. Einstein's theory said that gravity will bend light, and Newton's theory said that it will not. Careful observations of a solar eclipse showed Einstein's prediction to be right. Newton's physics was therefore falsified once and for all.

Thought Experiment: The Psychic

Imagine you are on a committee that reviews applications for funding new science projects. You are approached by a self-described psychic, who claims to be able to see the invisible "aura" that surrounds each person. On this basis, he can read personality traits such as passive or aggressive, shy or outgoing, arrogant or humble, and high or low self-esteem. He insists that his readings enable him to predict which occupation would be best for each person. Your fellow committee members are very impressed and want to fund his project. How would you try to verify the psychic's claim using Newton's method? How would you try to falsify it using Popper's method? Which is the better test?

To Popper, scientists are like gamblers: They make bets about what will happen to see which theories stand and which theories fall. He wrote:

> Confirmations should count only if they are the result of *risky predictions*; that is to say, if, unenlightened by the theory in question, we should have expected an event which was incompatible with the theory—an event which would have refuted the theory. . . . A theory which is not refutable by any conceivable event is non-scientific. Irrefutability is not a virtue of a theory (as people often think) but a vice. ... One can sum up all this by saying that *the criterion of the scientific status of a theory is its falsifiability, or refutability, or testability*. (From *Conjectures and Refutations*, by Karl Popper, 1976, pp. 36–37).

In Popper's view, if a theory is so "perfect" that it cannot be tested, then it is not science at all, but pseudoscience. The more tests a theory passes, the better the theory.

The disadvantage of falsification is that it can never tell us which claims are true once and for all. We have to keep weeding out bad theories and replacing them with better ones, never arriving at one final answer. For Popper, science is an unending search. Some people insist that this is the best we can do; others hold out with Newton for verification's ideal of certainty, even though it may be hard to achieve.

Fallacy Files

Post Hoc Ergo Propter Hoc

This fallacy occurs when someone concludes that one thing causes another just because it comes before it (the Latin phrase literally means "after the thing, therefore because of the thing"). For example, suppose you conclude that your flu symptoms have disappeared because of the expensive flu medication you have been taking for the past 4 days. You have no right to this conclusion, because most flu symptoms go away by themselves in 4 days. In this example, you were misled by a correlation—one thing happened after the other but not because of the other. Philosophers are careful to distinguish mere correlations from real causal relationships.

Reading Comprehension Questions

1. What is verification? Which philosopher advances this method?
2. What is falsification? Which philosopher advances this method?
3. Why does Newton frame no hypotheses?
4. Why can't we ever prove a theory true, according to Popper?
5. What is the thought experiment about the psychic designed to show? Explain.

Discussion Questions

1. Review the dialogue at the beginning of this chapter. Would Cameron agree more with Newton or Popper? What about Tonya? Give evidence.
2. Describe some hypotheses that you or people you know hold and explain why they cannot be tested.
3. Suppose someone you know claims his view is irrefutable (i.e., it "cannot be proven wrong"). Do you think this makes his view sound stronger or weaker?
4. In a study of heart disease, researchers interviewed thousands of heart attack victims and found that a significant number of them reported drinking six or more cups of coffee per day. Soon reporters started to publish stories claiming that "coffee causes heart attacks." Is this an example of post hoc ergo propter hoc? What tests would you like to see done before accepting the claim?

Essay Question

Do you believe there is a difference between genuine science and pseudoscience? Discuss both sides of this debate, making reference to Newton and Popper. Then, resolve the debate from your own point of view, presenting an argument in standard form for your conclusion.

Exercises

1. Write another dialogue between Tonya and Cameron. On this occasion, Tonya wants to buy some expensive diet pills based on the "before" and "after" pictures in the ads she sees, and Cameron argues that the pictures do not provide sufficient proof that the pills work.
2. Construct a thought experiment to test the claim that the theory that survives the most tests is the most worthy of belief.

Activities

1. Watch the movie *The Road to Wellville*, directed by Alan Parker (1994). What do you think it is trying to say about science and pseudoscience?
2. Obtain copies of the magazine *The Skeptical Inquirer* from your local library. Invite a group of classmates to help you make a presentation on some of the examples of pseudoscience examined in the magazine.
3. Identify beliefs held by friends and relatives that are clearly based on pseudoscience. Start a discussion with them about why they should or should not believe these things without further evidence.
4. Search out ads for foods and drugs that are either based on pseudoscience or commit post hoc ergo propter hoc, or both.
5. Research homeopathic medicine. Is this based on science or pseudoscience? What do you think accounts for its popularity?

References

Newton, I. (1962). *Philosophiae naturalis principia mathematica* (F. Cajori, Trans.). Berkeley, CA: University of California Press. (Original work published 1687)

Popper, K. (1976). *Conjectures and refutations*. London: Routledge & Kegan Paul Limited.

Further Reading

Derry, G. (1999). *What science is and how it works*. Princeton, NJ: Princeton University Press.

Dyson, F. (2004). *Infinite in all directions*. New York: Perennial.

Gardner, M. (1981). *Science—Good, bad, and bogus*. Amherst, NY: Prometheus Books.

Gardner, M. (1996). *Weird water and fuzzy logic*. Amherst, NY: Prometheus Books.

Huston, P. (1997). *Scams from the great beyond: How to make easy money off of ESP, astrology, UFOs, crop circles, cattle mutilations, alien abductions, Atlantis, channeling, and other new age nonsense*. Boulder CO: Paladin Press.

McCoy, B. (2000). *Quack! Tales of medical fraud*. Santa Monica, CA: Santa Monica Press.

Schick, T., & Vaughn, L. (2005). *How to think about weird things: Critical thinking for a new age*. Columbus, OH: McGraw Hill.

Shermer, M. (1995). *Why people believe weird things: Pseudoscience, superstition, and other confusions of our time*. New York: W. H. Freeman and Co.

PART 4

God

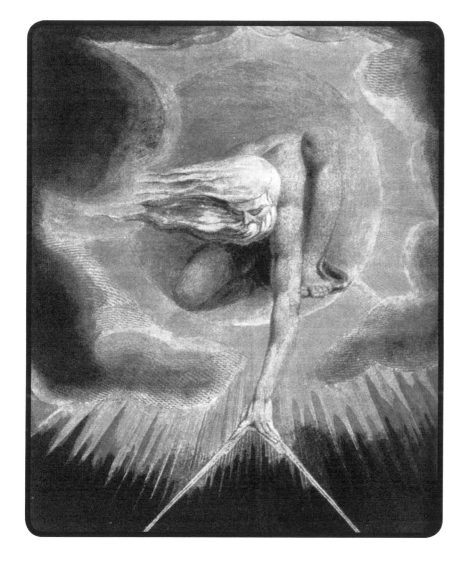

The Omnipotent, 1794,
William Blake

CHAPTER 13
Is the Natural World an Accident?

The Eyeball

Logan and Marissa are in biology class dissecting a pig's eyeball. Although they were initially grossed out by the assignment, they soon become fascinated.

MARISSA: OK, here's the iris. *<She pokes it with her scalpel.>*

LOGAN: *<Logan peers at the iris. Then, he reads from their worksheet.>* This is the part that opens and closes to let in light as needed.

MARISSA: Wow. *<She puts the scalpel down and wipes her hands.>* I never realized how complicated eyeballs are. I mean, I just took it for granted I could see in bright light and in dim light. I never realized what it took to make such a simple thing possible.

LOGAN: I know. And, this is just an eyeball. Think of all the other stuff going on in your body right now. Your brain thinking, your heart beating, your stomach digesting . . . All this stuff happening all by itself like some super high-tech machine.

MARISSA: It's better than any machine humans have ever made. *<She examines her own hand.>* It's hard to believe we evolved from nothing but mud and protein.

LOGAN: *<Leaning toward her and lowering his voice>* You really believe that?

MARISSA: Evolution? Sure. It's scientifically proven. *<She pulls her biology textbook out of her bag.>* There's no denying the evidence we read about last week.

LOGAN: Come on, that's just a theory, and it's full of holes. *<He takes her book and sets it on the table.>* There's no way mud and protein could change into a human.

MARISSA: That's not what evolution says, Logan. There were thousands of steps and it took millions of years. It's not just a theory, it's a fact—because we witness evolution in real time when viruses like AIDS evolve.

LOGAN: Well, I'm not saying evolution never happened. I'm just saying it doesn't account for everything. *<He folds his arms on his chest.>* Only God is intelligent and powerful enough to design all of nature.

MARISSA: But, is nature really a design? I mean, there are so many defects. If God made humans special, then why do we have an appendix? We never use it for anything. All it does is get infected and then you have to go to the hospital to have it taken out. To me, that's evidence that we evolved from a lower life form.

LOGAN: Maybe to some extent. I think God works through evolution. See, he didn't make us perfect from the beginning because he wanted us to improve over time.

MARISSA: Could be. But, I don't see any role for God to play. *<She picks up her scalpel preparing to make another incision.>* It's pretty clear nature can take care of itself.

Questions

- Why does Logan think nature was designed by God?
- Why doesn't Marissa think so?
- With whom do you agree more, and why?
- What is a design? Is nature a design in your view?

- Is it possible for something that looks like a design to come about by accident? If not, why? If so, give an example.

Is the Natural World an Accident?

Most people experience a sense of awe and wonder when they contemplate the natural world. Think about a sunset over the ocean that streaks the sky with purple and gold, or a grove of sweet-smelling orange trees, or a roaring lion. Nature is truly gorgeous. But the most amazing thing of all is how it forms a functioning system. Evaporation from the ocean causes rain, which makes plants grow; plants make oxygen for animals to breathe and food for them to eat; animals reproduce generation after generation, and the chain keeps going. It seems like one huge orchestrated play—all of the actors playing their parts in harmony. For many people, the complex beauty of the natural world proves that there must be a God who made it. The following thought experiment tests this claim.

Thought Experiment: Target Practice

Suppose you are an alien flying through outer space in a fast rocket ship. For a long time you see nothing but blackness and tiny specks of light outside your window. Then, suddenly your ship enters our solar system, and slows down near the planet Mars. As you orbit around it, you see nothing but swirling dust and giant craters. You consider blowing it up just for fun and to practice using your new weapons system. But just then the planet Earth catches your eye. As you approach it, you see clouds floating across vast patches of blue water and green land. Closer still, you can make out little snowcapped mountains, winding rivers, and beach-rimmed islands. Do you think you would be just as tempted to blow up this planet? Do you think it would occur to you that this planet had been deliberately made by someone for a special purpose? Explain your answers.

Could a planet as complex and beautiful as Earth have come about by accident? The English theologian William Paley (1743–1805) answered "no" to that question. Arguing that God must have created Earth, Paley proposed an analogy between nature

William Paley
(1743–1805)

and a watch: Have you ever looked at the mechanism inside an old-fashioned watch or clock? You can see dials, springs, and levers moving in rhythm to keep time. (Today's digital timepieces are even more sophisticated, though it's harder to see all of the little parts in action.) A watch is an impressive system—so many little parts work together to make the hands go around.

Paley was struck by how much a watch resembles nature. All the different elements of our ecosystems work together to make the world go around. No one would ever think that a watch had come about by accident. On the contrary, you can tell just by looking at it that a watch is designed for a purpose. So, likewise, no one should think the natural world came about by accident either. Paley concluded that the natural world shows signs of purpose just as surely as the watch does. Because the watch has a designer, the world must have a designer, too. He wrote:

> Every indication of contrivance, every manifestation of design, which existed in the watch, exists in the works of Nature; with the difference, on the side of Nature, of being greater and more, and that in a degree which exceeds all computation. I mean, that the contrivances of Nature surpass the contrivances of art, in the complexity, subtlety, and curiosity of the mechanism; and still more, if possible, do they go beyond them in number and variety; yet, a multitude of cases, are not less evidently mechanical, not less evidently contrivances, not less evidently accommodated to their end, or suited to their office, than are the most perfect productions of human ingenuity. (From *Natural Theology* by William Paley, 1800, [http://www-phil.tamu.edu/~gary/intro/paper.paley.html])

Paley's view is called *creationism* because it holds that only God could create a mechanistic system as complex and beautiful as Earth and its inhabitants.

Richard Dawkins (1941–) is an English biologist who finds Paley's argument unconvincing. Paley proposed his analogy before scientists discovered the theory of *evolution*, according to which all life on our planet developed from basic chemical ingredients over a period of millions and millions of years. Dawkins argues that if you understand evolution correctly you'll see that the natural world is not like a watch, and there's no reason to suppose that there exists a God who created it.

Richard Dawkins
(1941–)

Here's a simple example of how evolution works: A colony of tiny fish is swimming around in a pond eating scum floating on the water. As they continue to eat, their supply begins to run out. The fish are also reproducing, however, and reproduction creates diversity among them. Some fish are born with overdeveloped fins that enable them to propel themselves onto the shore where they have access to more food. Before long, all the fish with small fins die of starvation. Meanwhile, the fish with big fins thrive and produce offspring with even bigger fins. Finally the fins are so big that they function as legs. The resulting animals look as though they were designed to walk on land, but really their legs are just defective fins.

Although many people today accept the theory of evolution, they tend to suspect that this process could not have occurred all by itself. They assert that if God had not started and guided the process, it would never have had such a successful result. According to Dawkins, however, this assertion reveals a lack of understanding. Evolution has resulted in such a complex and beautiful world because of the survival of the fittest. Of course the result is successful—any life forms that were not successful died out! Evolution has produced impressive survivors who work together so effectively that it *looks like* someone designed them for a purpose.

Dawkins maintains that there is no role for God to play in the story of evolution. Every batch of offspring has new features. If these features happen to work well in the environment, then they are passed on to the next generation. If these features happen to work poorly, then the offspring die out without passing anything on. So, the impressive results we see are actually caused by defect, suffering, and death. Dawkins writes:

> During the minute it takes me to compose this sentence, thousands of animals are being eaten alive; others are running for their lives, whimpering with fear; others are being slowly devoured from within by rasping parasites; thousands of all kids are dying of starvation, thirst, and disease. It must be so. If there is ever a time of plenty, this very fact will automatically lead to an increase in population until the natural state of starvation and misery is restored. . . . In a universe of blind physical forces and genetic replication, some people are going to get hurt, other people are going to get lucky, and you won't find any rhyme or reason in it, or any justice. The universe we observe has precisely the properties we should expect if there is, at bottom, no design, no purpose, no evil and no good, nothing but blind, pitiless indifference. (From *River Out of Eden: A Darwinian View of Life* by Richard Dawkins, 1995, pp. 132–3)

Although it is *possible* that there is a God or creator who works through evolution, Dawkins concludes that it doesn't seem likely. Evolution alone is sufficient to explain what we see.

Dawkins insists that believing in evolution is not the same as believing that the natural world came about "by accident" because the process involves so many steps and takes such a long time. Nevertheless, evolution works through chance occurrences every step of the way. If Dawkins is right, then there is no ultimate purpose to life on Earth. The natural world is nothing but an extraordinary coincidence of favorable conditions. Critics worry that this outlook renders human existence meaningless.

Many people think philosophy is boring and irrelevant to daily life. This cannot be said about the debate between creationism and evolution, however. Some people feel that evolution undermines faith and morality and therefore should not be taught in schools. Others feel it must be taught everywhere as one of the most important discoveries of Western history. This controversy often appears on the news and provokes a great deal of emotional discussion. It is to be hoped that philosophy will help people understand each other and come to agreement some day. In any case, very little in biology today makes any sense except in light of evolution.

Fallacy Files

Straw Man

Charles Darwin was the English scientist who first published the theory of evolution about 150 years ago. Many people were shocked and insulted by Darwin's assertion that human beings and apes evolved from a common ancestor. Newspapers carried headlines such as the following: "According to Darwin, Your Grandmother Was a Monkey!" Although these headlines may have been amusing, they also misled a lot of people by oversimplifying Darwin's view. Philosophers consider such oversimplification an instance of the "straw man" fallacy. A straw man is a scarecrow. Anyone can set up a straw man and knock it down. Not many people can knock down a real man, however. So, if you want to make an effective criticism against an opponent, you should make sure that you take on their true view, not just an oversimplified version of it.

Reading Comprehension Questions

1. What is creationism? Which philosopher holds this view?
2. What is evolution? Which philosopher holds this view?
3. Why does a watch resemble nature, according to Paley?
4. Why is there no role for God to play in the story of evolution, according to Dawkins?
5. What claim is the thought experiment about target practice designed to test? Explain.

Discussion Questions

1. Review the dialogue at the beginning of this chapter. Would Logan agree more with Paley or Dawkins? What about Marissa? Give evidence.
2. Describe an example of survival of the fittest you have seen for yourself.
3. How do college entrance exams resemble the process of natural selection?
4. Give an example of something that might be hard for evolution alone to explain. Why do you think it might be hard?
5. Why do you think some people feel that evolution undermines faith and morality? Do you agree? Explain.

Essay Question

Do you believe the natural world was designed for a purpose? Discuss both sides of this debate, making reference to Paley and Dawkins. Then, resolve the debate from your own point of view, presenting an argument in standard form for your conclusion.

Exercises

1. Write a dialogue between Daquan and Carina. Daquan argues that a design is a pattern that is made deliberately by someone. Carina gives examples to show this definition is inadequate.
2. Construct a thought experiment to test the claim that you can tell whether or not something is designed for a purpose by looking at it.

Activities

1. Watch the PBS film *Evolution Part 1: Darwin's Dangerous Idea*, written and directed by David Espar and Susan K. Lewis (2001). How did Darwin discover evolution and why was he reluctant to publish his discovery?
2. Go out and observe the natural world, making a list of things you see as defects. What makes them defects? Why do you think they exist?
3. Write a report on the controversy concerning the teaching of evolution in public schools. What is your position on this issue?
4. Make a paper snowflake. Is a real snowflake a design or an accident?
5. Interview your biology teacher about evolution. Does it conflict with faith in God in his or her view? Why or why not?

References

Dawkins, R. (1995). *River out of Eden: A Darwinian view of life.* New York, NY: Basic Books.

Paley, W. (n.d.). *Natural theology.* Retrieved April 30, 2007, from http://www-phil.tamu.edu/~gary/intro/paper.paley.html (Original work published 1800)

Further Reading

Dembski, W. A., & Ruse, M. (Eds.). (2004). *Debating design: From Darwin to DNA.* Cambridge, England: Cambridge University Press.

Gould, S. J. (1999). *Rocks of ages: Science and religion in the fullness of life.* New York: Ballantine.

Hume, D. (n.d.). *Dialogues concerning natural religion.* Retrieved April 30, 2007, from http://www.philosophyofreligion.info/humedcnr.html (Original work published 1779)

Moody, T. (2001). Intelligent design: A catechism. *Philosophy Now, 31,* 32–45.

Plantinga, A. (2000). *Warranted Christian belief.* Oxford, England: Oxford University Press.

Ruse, M. (1998). Answering the creationists: Where they go wrong—and what they're afraid of. *Free-Inquiry, 18*(2), 28–32.

Swinburne, R. (2002). Arguments from design. *Think: Philosophy for Everyone, 1,* 199–212.

Zimmer, C. (2001). *Evolution: The triumph of an idea.* New York: HarperCollins.

CHAPTER 14
Is It Reasonable to Believe?

The Boyfriend

Jill and Jennifer go to different schools, and they just met at a party. After talking about friends they have in common, they realize that they recently dated the same guy, Bryan. Both of them broke up with him, but for different reasons.

JILL: You know what Bryan and I fought the most about?

JENNIFER: *<Sipping from her drink>* What?

JILL: God. *<She pops a pretzel into her mouth.>*

JENNIFER: Hey, that's what he and I fought most about too!

JILL: *<Smirking at the memory>* Yeah, it drove me crazy how he wouldn't take a stand.

JENNIFER: *<Rolling her eyes>* I know! I kept asking him, Bryan, when are you going to grow up and start coming to church?

JILL: *<Suddenly embarrassed>* Oh! So, you're a believer. I'm not. *<She blushes.>* I just thought Bryan should make up his mind one way or another. I mean, even though he wouldn't go to church, he always said a prayer at night. He figured, just in case it turns out that God exists, he wanted to be sure he would get into heaven.

JENNIFER: Yeah, clever little rascal isn't he? Somehow, I don't think God's going to let someone in who says "just in case" prayers. I mean, you have to really believe to get into heaven. <*Gives Jill a quizzical look*> But, you don't believe. Aren't you worried about what will happen to you when you die?

JILL: Not really, no. There's no proof of the existence of God or life after death.

JENNIFER: Yeah, but there's no proof against these beliefs either! I believe in God and that when I die my soul will go to heaven. I think these are good beliefs, even though I admit I can't prove them. If I'm wrong, and death really is the end, I guess I'll never know it. So, there's no harm done.

JILL: <*Shaking her head sadly*> But, you're harming yourself right now. Think about all the time you're wasting in church. And, who knows what kind of experiences you could be having if you weren't worried about contradicting your religion.

JENNIFER: But, I actually enjoy going to church and living according to religious values.

JILL: <*Closing her eyes in reverie*> Yeah, I can see why it might be nice to have heaven to look forward to, especially during bad times. <*She opens her eyes.*> But, I think you work harder to avoid bad times when you don't believe. I figure, because this life is all I've got I'm going to make the best of it. Do you . . .

JENNIFER: <*Interrupting her in a loud whisper*> Hey look at that! Bryan just walked in. Do you think he's still trying to have it both ways?

Questions

- What are Jennifer's reasons for believing in God and an afterlife?
- What are Jill's reasons for rejecting these beliefs?
- With whom do you agree more, and why?
- What is Bryan's position?

- Describe a time when you couldn't decide which side to take on an issue. Did you eventually take a side? Why or why not?

To Believe or Not Believe

Why do people believe in God? As noted in the previous chapter, some people find evidence of God in nature; others find it in personal experiences. Other people, however, believe in God even though they admit that there isn't sufficient evidence of his existence. This view is called *fideism* (from the Latin word for faith). Fideists believe that God deliberately hides himself so that humans have to rely on faith rather than evidence.

Fideism is a puzzle for philosophers because there is no way to test it, to prove it, *or* disprove it. Suppose your friend Katie tells you she thinks there's a dragon in her basement because she hears noises at night. You go down into the basement to check, and you see nothing. You conclude that the dragon does not exist, but Katie concludes that the dragon is invisible. Clearly Katie has decided to believe in this dragon no matter what. She doesn't want to hear other explanations for the noises. She just wants to keep her belief. This attitude seems stubborn and unreasonable—this is how fideists seem to many philosophers.

However, the French philosopher Blaise Pascal (1623–1662) provided an ingenious defense of fideism. He argued that it is reasonable to believe in God even though his existence cannot be proven. Pascal's particular view is known as *voluntarism,* the view that sometimes you are justified in believing something because you want to believe that thing. Like many philosophers of his time, Pascal was also a brilliant scientist and mathematician (an important early computer language was named after him). As a young adult he was not religious because he didn't think there was sufficient evidence of the existence of God. In fact, he hung out with a bunch of other scientists and mathematicians who were secretly atheists. They loved to gamble and didn't see any point in going to church.

Then one day, Pascal had a change of heart. He suddenly became a passionate believer. He was tired of the despair caused by the thought of living in a godless and uncaring world. However, he was a bit embarrassed by his newly found faith because he

Blaise Pascal
(1623–1662)

knew he had no more reason for believing in God now than he did before. He wanted to find a way to explain to his atheist friends why it is reasonable to believe without evidence.

Before his conversion, Pascal had been developing a branch of mathematics that would come to be known as *game theory*. Game theory is a system of formulas used to calculate the conditions of rational risk taking. For example, banks use it today to determine safe investments. Pascal and his friends used it to make a lot of money gambling. Suppose someone asks you to bet on a coin toss: heads or tails. If you bet heads, and you are right, you get $100; if you bet tails and you are right, you get $1. If you are wrong betting either way, then you get nothing. Which way should you bet?

Even if you are in the habit of picking tails, a little reflection should tell you that the only rational choice is to bet heads. You have nothing to lose, and everything to gain.

Pascal argued that deciding whether or not to be religious is a bet just like this one. He argued that whether or not God really exists, the rational course is to bet on the existence of God. If you bet on God and you are right, you get eternal life, as well as hope and fellowship in this life. Even if God does not exist, you at least get the hope and fellowship in this life. If you bet against God and you are right, then all you get is this life, which Pascal found depressing. If you bet against God and you are wrong then you add the risk of some sort of punishment from God to the despair caused by thinking you live in a Godless world. You have nothing to lose and everything to gain by betting on God.

Notice that Pascal is not proving that God exists any more than he is proving that the coin will land on heads. As far as he's concerned, it's a 50/50 chance. But, Pascal determined that believing is just like making a bet, and betting on God has a far better payoff whatever the fact of the matter turns out to be. In fact, he thought that because the payoff of eternal life in heaven is infinite, it is rational to bet on God even if there is less than a 50/50 chance that he exists. Pascal wrote:

> Let us then examine this point, and say, "God is, or He is not." But to which side shall we incline? Reason can decide nothing here. There is an infinite chaos which separates us. A game is being played at the extremity of this infinite distance where heads or tails will turn up. What will you wager? According to reason, you can do neither the one

thing nor the other; according to reason, you can defend neither of the propositions. . . . —Yes, but you must wager. It is not optional. You are embarked. Which will you chose then? . . . Let us weigh the gain and the loss in wagering that God is. Let us estimate these two chances. If you gain, you gain all; if you lose, you lose nothing. Wager then without hesitation that He is. (From *Pensées*, by Blaise Pascal, 1670/1958, p. 66)

A wager is a bet; hence this argument has come to be known as Pascal's Wager.

Pascal's Wager is appealing. There is no doubt that many people say prayers or attend church because they believe that there is a chance they may be rewarded with eternal life. But, are there any holes in the argument?

Notice that by comparing religious belief to a bet, Pascal implied that you have to be either a theist, someone who definitely believes God exists, or an atheist, someone who definitely believes God does not exist. This ignores the third possibility of agnosticism. Agnostics maintain that because there is no definite proof for or against the existence of God, we should not take a stand on either side. To some people, agnosticism looks like an excuse for not making up your mind. But, agnostics insist that their approach is the most honest. For example, suppose your car won't start. When you call the garage, they ask you what the problem is so they know what kind of help to send. Should you take a wild guess or simply admit you don't know?

Pascal insists that we must make up our minds and place our bets. But, what if God punishes gamblers and gives eternal life to those who are honest enough to admit that they don't know? The point here is simply that, because Pascal doesn't know how God decides who gets into heaven, he cannot rule out agnosticism as the best choice.

Furthermore, many philosophers worry that by focusing so much on how to get into heaven, people lose sight of what's important in this life. In his *Thus spoke Zarathustra*, (1974) the 19th-century philosopher Friedrich Nietzsche presents a thought experiment like the one below to help you determine whether or not you're making the most out of this life.

Before the modern era it was very rare to question the existence of God. By the 19th century, however, philosophers such as Nietzsche began to argue that religious belief is actually harm-

Thought Experiment:
The Eternal Recurrence

Suppose you just found out that, when you die, you are reborn as a baby and have to live the exact same life all over again. Would you be happy to hear this news? How about living the same life over and over again for all eternity? Does that sound like fun or does it sound like a nightmare? Your answer tells you a lot about how happy you are. Usually, if you enjoy something, you are happy to do it all over again— especially if you don't remember that you've done it before. Think about it: How much of the last 24 hours would you be willing to do again right now? If the answer is "not much," why do you feel this way? Is it good to live in a way that you would never want to relive? What changes would you need to make to your life to increase the amount of time you would be willing to relive?

At the end of his book *The Republic*, Plato discusses the idea of being reborn again after death. But, in this case, each soul is permitted to choose the next life they will lead. Plato ridicules those who choose to be rich and powerful because he is convinced that they will ultimately lead unhappy, worthless lives. He admires the great warrior Odysseus, who chooses the life of a simple citizen for his next life. Why do you think Odysseus makes this choice? What life would you choose? (Plato's *Republic*, Book X)

ful. Nietzsche finds the traditional Christian image of Christ as shepherd to his flock very telling: sheep are rather stupid and will blindly follow the shepherd, even to the slaughterhouse. In a similar vein, Karl Marx (1818–1883) wrote that religion is the opium of the people. He saw belief in God as a tool used by the ruling classes to keep the working class in submission. His analogy with opium is meant to suggest that religion is a kind of drug that keeps us in check.

The Austrian psychologist Sigmund Freud (1856–1939) also believed religion is dangerous and made an interesting argument against fideism. *Psychology* is the scientific study of the workings of the human mind. Freud was a pioneer in this field. In his view, psychology proves that religious faith is an illusion born of our ignorance about the world and the insecurity that this causes.

Freud was best known for discovering the subconscious. The subconscious is a hidden source of desires deep within our minds. Although we are not aware of subconscious desires, they control much of what we think and do. For example, people often don't know why they find themselves attracted to certain people and not to others. We often can find an explanation, however, by examin-

Sigmund Freud
(1856–1939)

ing early life experiences. You might easily fall in love with someone who indirectly resembles one of your parents or your favorite babysitter. According to Freud, childhood experiences shape the choices we make later in life in ways we never realize.

Freud argued that the subconscious is the part of us that never really grows up. It is the part of us that wants to cry like a baby and be coddled and spoiled. He believed religious faith is a product of this infantile thinking. Belief in God is nothing but a hidden desire to have a perfect father who could solve all of our problems for us and keep us safe forever. Those who believe are giving in to their inner child. The result is an unhealthy and immature way of coping with the hardships of everyday life.

According to Freud, faith is a subconscious desire to escape the truth. In his view, scientific thinkers will reject the illusion of heaven, which he compares to a "mirage of wide acres in the moon." He wrote:

> You are afraid, perhaps, that [atheists] will not be able to stand up to the hard test? Well, let us at least hope they will. . . . Their scientific knowledge has taught them much since the days of the Deluge, and it will increase their power still further. And, as for the great necessities of Fate, against which there is no help, they will learn to endure them with resignation. Of what use to them is the mirage of wide acres in the moon, whose harvest no one has ever yet seen? As honest smallholders on this earth they will know how to cultivate their plot in such a way that it supports them. By withdrawing their expectations from the other world and concentrating all their liberated energies into their life on earth, they will probably succeed in achieving a state of things in which life will become tolerable for everyone and civilization no longer oppressive to anyone. (From *The Future of an Illusion*, by Sigmund Freud, 1927/1964, p. 82)

Freud believed that religion will inevitably die out with the advance of science.

All three of the last thinkers we looked at, Nietzsche, Marx, and Freud, would insist that without the promise of a reward in the afterlife, people would not put up with injustices in this life. With only one life to live, they would want to make this life as good as possible. Pascal, in contrast, would insist that only the promise of an eternal reward will motivate people to fight injustice. Historically, most of the people who have dedicated their lives to making a better world have been motivated by belief in God. Clearly, both sides of this debate are worthy of further investigation.

Fallacy Files

Rhetorical Question

A rhetorical question is a question that is really a disguised declarative statement. For example, if the teacher says "Do you want me to send you to the principal's office?" what she means is "You will be sent to the principal's office for discipline if you don't behave." Although the use of rhetorical questions may work with misbehaving children, it is not a good way to make a philosophical point. For example, suppose you believe the government should ensure that all citizens have access to health care. You may be tempted to say, "Who wouldn't pay a few extra tax dollars to ensure their neighbor's health?" But, this would be a mistake because the effect will be to pressure your opponents into agreement against their will. Instead, take a bit more time to say what the costs and benefits will be, and why you think that the benefits are worth the cost. Good philosophers try to win the argument through reason rather than coercion.

Reading Comprehension Questions

1. What is fideism? Which philosopher holds this view?
2. What is psychology? Which philosopher represents this discipline?
3. Why is believing in God like a reasonable bet, according to Pascal?
4. Why is believing in God a dangerous illusion, according to Freud?
5. What is the thought experiment about the eternal recurrence designed to show? Explain.

Discussion Questions

1. Review the dialogue at the beginning of this chapter. Would Jill agree more with Pascal or Freud? What about Jennifer? Give evidence.
2. Is it possible that psychology explains the form religion takes without showing that religious faith is baseless?
3. Is it possible that there is a devil who gives an eternal life of bliss to everyone that refuses to believe in God? If not, why not? If so, who should you believe in, God or the devil?
4. If God exists, why do you suppose he makes it so hard for human beings to know whether he exists or not?

Essay Question

Do you believe it is reasonable to believe in God and the afterlife without evidence? Discuss both sides of this debate, making reference to Pascal and Freud. Then, resolve the debate from your own point of view, presenting an argument in standard form for your conclusion.

Exercises

1. Write a dialogue between Bjorn and Sylvie. Bjorn argues that going to church isn't worth it. Sylvie argues that it is.
2. Construct a thought experiment to test the claim that going to church is harmless.

Activities

1. Watch the movie *Groundhog Day*, directed by Harold Ramis (1993). How does its plot relate to the thought experiment about the eternal recurrence?
2. Research stories of reincarnation and assess the scientific evidence for them.

3. Conduct an anonymous survey about people's religious beliefs (or lack thereof). Be sure to include "don't know" and "don't care" options.
4. Make up a religion that is not subject to the criticisms of Freud and Marx.
5. Write a letter to a friend or relative who has some behaviors of which you disapprove. Use the myth of the eternal recurrence to try to convince that person to change behaviors.

References

Freud, S. (1964). *The future of an illusion.* (J. Strachey, Trans.). Garden City, NY: Doubleday Anchor. (Original work published 1927)

Marx, K. (2006). Contribution to the critique of Hegel's philosophy of right. In O*n religion* (pp. 41–58). Atlanta: Scholars Press (Original work written in 1843)

Nietzsche, F. (1974). *Thus spoke Zarathustra* (R. J. Hollingdale, Trans). Baltimore: Penguin. (Original work published 1885)

Pascal, B. (1958). *Pensées* (W. F. Trotter, Trans.). New York: Dutton. (Original work published 1670)

Further Reading

Freud, S. (1961). *Civilization and its discontents.* New York: Norton (Original work published 1930)

Nagel, T. (1986). *The view from nowhere.* New York: Oxford University Press.

Nietzsche, F. (1967). *The will to power* (W. Kaufmann & R. J. Hollingdale, Trans.). New York: Random House. (Original work published in 1901)

Nietzsche, F. (2001). *The gay science* (J. Nauckhoff, Trans.). New York: Cambridge University Press. (Original work published 1882)

Roach, M. (2005). *Spook: Science tackles the afterlife.* New York: Norton.

CHAPTER 15
What Is the Meaning of Life?

The Chore

Shannon is walking down the street when she sees Devon mowing his backyard. She calls his name. He pauses for a moment and waves to her. Then, he returns to his work. Shannon is about to continue on her way, but she changes her mind and dashes across the yard to him.

SHANNON: *<Shouting>* How's it going, Devon? *<She waits for him to turn and look.>* It seems like you're always mowin' this yard.

DEVON: *<Stopping the mower, wiping his brow>* Yeah. Every week.

SHANNON: What a drag! All that work and then it doesn't even keep. You have to do it over and over again. That would make me crazy!

DEVON: I dunno. It's just like anything else. *<He kneels to retie his shoelace.>* Like, you spend all night studying for a test and you're so happy to have it done, but there's another one just around the corner. Or, how it takes an hour to get all showered, shaved, dressed, and ready in the morning, but you have to do it all over again the next day. Nothing really lasts.

SHANNON: *<Sitting on the grass>* I don't see it that way. The tests we take are leading to graduation. And, it matters how you look—like, for making friends and getting a good job. All that stuff adds up.

DEVON: <*Stretching out on the grass beside her*> What—graduate, get married, buy a house, and have a kid so he can mow the yard?

SHANNON: Well . . . maybe. <*She bursts out laughing.*> Yeah, OK. What's so bad about that? <*She punches his arm.*>

DEVON: <*Cringing*> I didn't say there was anything bad about it. It just proves everything is ultimately pointless.

SHANNON: <*Alarmed*> Why pointless? If reaching those goals makes me happy, then that's the point. The point is to be happy.

DEVON: <*Looking at her thoughtfully*> Are you happy now?

SHANNON: Not especially. But once I graduate, get married, buy a house, and have a kid who can mow the yard I will be. <*She grins.*>

DEVON: <*Nodding slowly with a grim look on his face*> Sure.

SHANNON: Look, maybe the point of the whole thing is to get to heaven some day. <*She lies back on the grass and gazes up at the sky.*> That would definitely make even mowing the lawn worthwhile.

Questions

- Why does Devon think life is pointless?
- Why does Shannon think life has a point?
- With whom do you agree more, and why?
- Do you ever feel that you do the same things over and over again? Name some examples.
- Do you consider yourself happy? Why or why not.
- What is the point of life in your view? Explain.

The Meaning of Life

Everyone experiences moments when life seems empty and futile. If it happens during your forties and causes you to buy a red sports car, it's called a "mid-life crisis." But most people don't wait until mid life to question their own existence. Why go on? Does anything really matter? Questioning along these lines is a common cause of depression, anxiety, and even suicide. The 20th-century philosopher Albert Camus (1913–1960) suggested that suicide, the problem of whether life is worth it or not, is the only real philosophical problem.

Albert Camus
(1913–1960)

Camus is part of a movement of the last two centuries called *existentialism*. Existentialists get their name from their preoccupation with the existential crisis described above. Although many people try to ignore it or cover it up, existentialists boldly face it and try to find solutions. According to Camus, once you notice how repetitive life is, you have to admit that your existence is pointless. Think about it: You get up, go to school or work, come home, and go to bed, only to do the same thing again tomorrow. You may sometimes feel as though you are making progress toward something, but you eventually discover that you never really get there. Camus made his point through the ancient Greek myth in the following thought experiment.

Thought Experiment: The Myth of Sisyphus

Suppose you wake up one morning to find the gods are angry with you. They have decided to sentence you to an eternal life of punishment. The first thing they require you to do is roll a boulder to the top of a mountain. The boulder is so heavy it takes you many weeks to reach the  top. When you finally make it you feel relieved and even a little proud of yourself for accomplishing your task. The gods are not impressed, however. They immediately send the boulder back to the bottom of the mountain and command you to roll it up again. At that moment the horror of your fate becomes clear: You are condemned to roll the same rock to the top of the same mountain over and over again forever. How would this make you feel? Is this a good metaphor for life? Why or why not?

Søren Kierkegaard
(1813–1855)

Søren Kierkegaard (1813–1855) was a 19th-century Danish existentialist. He was a young man in love when he experienced his existential crisis. The girl of his dreams was named Regina. Kierkegaard wrote her beautiful love poetry, and she returned his affections. He came to feel so passionately about this girl that he asked her to be his wife. Even though he knew she would marry him, he soon decided he could not go through with the wedding. He realized that what he truly loved was an idealistic picture of Regina that he had in his mind. The real Regina, being an ordinary human, would never live up to this ideal. So, he broke off the engagement—although he hated himself for doing it—and he soon became suicidal.

For Kierkegaard, questions about the meaning of existence lead to questions about God. He wrote:

> My life has been brought to an impasse, I loathe existence, it is without savor, lacking salt and sense. . . . I stick my finger into existence—it smells of nothing. Where am I? Who am I? How came I here? What is this thing called "the world"? What does this word mean? Who is it that has lured me into the thing, and now leaves me there? Who am I? How did I come into the world? Why was I not consulted? . . . How did I obtain an interest in this big enterprise they call reality? Why should I have an interest in it? Is it not a voluntary concern? And if I am to be compelled to take part in it, where is the director? I should like to make a remark to him. (From *Repetition*, by Søren Kierkegaard, 1843/1941, p. 114)

Although Kierkegaard started out angry with God for making life so difficult, he eventually realized that God is the only true solution to the existential crisis every human being must face.

In Kierkegaard's view, God is the only being who lives up to the idealistic picture we have of him in our minds. Therefore, according to Kierkegaard, God is the only thing worthy of our love. Kierkegaard was convinced that the main problem with human life is that we develop passionate desires for things that don't last. Every time we lose something we love, our hearts break a little bit. This happens over and over again until we are lost in despair. God is the only thing that lasts forever. Kierkegaard insists therefore that the only way to avoid despair is to love God and God alone with all your strength. Because of his religious orientation, Kierkegaard is known as the first Christian existentialist.

One problem with Kierkegaard's solution, however, is that his ideal of God may be just as artificial as his image of Regina. When Kierkegaard fell in love with Regina, he was caught up in a fantasy in his own imagination. How do we know God is not just another fantasy? Many people would rather face the truth—even if the truth is depressing—than live in a dream world.

Richard Taylor (1919–2003) was an American philosopher who looked for a solution to the existential crisis without resorting to God. In Taylor's view, people come to believe life is meaningless when they feel like nothing comes of what they do. But, according to Taylor, this feeling is based on a misunderstanding. Although it is true that the accomplishments we strive after fade, these accomplishments are not the point of the striving. Rather, the striving itself is the point. The truth is that we would die of boredom if we accomplished all of our goals once and for all! Conceiving new goals and working toward them is what by nature human beings do best. Taylor believed that the most valuable thing that comes of our striving is the enjoyment of being human and living a human life. In order to illustrate his point, Taylor retold the myth of Sisyphus, summed up in the paragraph below.

Richard Taylor
(1919–2003)

Imagine the gods have watched you rolling that boulder up the mountain for a while and begin to feel sorry for you. They decide to cast a spell on you so that you have one and only one desire in life, namely, to roll the same boulder up the same mountain. Whereas before you dreaded your fate because you had no desire to roll the boulder—now you're happy because you're doing exactly what you want to do. You can't think of any better way to spend your time, and you'd be very disappointed if the gods made you stop.

Would your life have meaning now? Taylor thought it would, and he thought this version of the myth provides a good metaphor for life. Granted—our daily routines are repetitive, and we may not accomplish anything in the end, but that shouldn't stop us from having a good time. We don't need any kind of special point for our lives any more than worms or birds do. Taylor wrote:

> You no sooner drew your first breath than you responded to the will that was in you to live. You no more ask whether it will be worthwhile, or whether anything of significance will come of it than the worms or the birds. The point of living is simply to be living, in the manner that it is your nature to be living. You go through life building your castles, each of

these beginning to fade into time as the next is begun; yet it would be no salvation to rest from all this. . . . The meaning of life is from within us, it is not bestowed from without, and it far exceeds in both its beauty and permanence any heaven of which men have ever dreamed or yearned for. (From "The Meaning of Life," by Richard Taylor, 2004, p. 27–8)

Non-religious existentialists like Taylor stress the importance of investing ourselves in our daily routines rather than always looking forward to a better future.

Taylor's solution to the existential crisis is attractive in so far as it suggests human beings already have everything they need within themselves to be happy. But, this raises an important question: Why aren't more people happy more often? Taylor makes it sound easy to enjoy life. If they are honest, however, many people will admit they find this very difficult. First of all, the goals that determine our daily routines often are not the goals we choose for ourselves. For example, students rarely get much choice as to which school to attend. It is hard to enjoy earning a diploma from a school you don't like. Yet, even when we choose our own goals, we often find them too hard to reach. For example, many people want to be physically fit but can't find time and energy to exercise and eat right. So, it is not clear whether Taylor is correct to say that working toward goals is what human beings by nature do best.

Perhaps Taylor would say that striving wouldn't be striving if it were easy. He might insist that there are things we can do to make our daily routines manageable and even fun. But, Kierkegaard would still worry that Taylor is missing the underlying unifying principle for life that God provides. As with all of the issues we have discussed in this book, it is up to you to decide where the truth lies.

Reading Comprehension Questions

1. What is Christian existentialism? Which philosopher holds this view?
2. What is non-religious existentialism? Which philosopher holds this view?

> ### Fallacy Files
>
> ### *Non Sequitur*
>
> *Non sequitur* is a Latin phrase that means "it doesn't follow." Philosophers use this phrase to point out instances where someone makes a leap in logic. In a good argument, each point leads to the next so that if you follow it step-by-step you arrive unavoidably at the conclusion. If the argument skips a step, then there is no reason to accept its conclusion. For example, suppose someone says, "I need a summer job. Lawn mowing is a summer job. Therefore, I need to mow lawns." The philosophical response to this logic would be "Non sequitur!" There is no reason to accept the conclusion because there may be other summer jobs. In order for this argument to work it would need to add a step asserting that lawn mowing is the *only* summer job available. Avoiding non sequiturs helps us think more clearly and speak more persuasively.

3. Why is loving God the only way to avoid despair, according to Kierkegaard?
4. What is the point of striving for accomplishments, according to Taylor?
5. What is the myth of Sisyphus thought experiment designed to show? Explain.

Discussion Questions

1. Review the dialogue at the beginning of this chapter. Would Shannon agree more with Kierkegaard or Taylor? What about Devon? Give evidence.
2. Do you think Kierkegaard made the right choice breaking his engagement to Regina? What would you have done?
3. Do you think most people enjoy their daily routines? Do you? What would Taylor say about those who do not?
4. Do you find it hard to be happy? Why or why not? What do you think it would take to make you happy once and for all?

Essay Question

Do you believe that God is necessary to make life meaningful? Discuss both sides of this debate, making reference to Kierkegaard and Taylor. Then, resolve the debate from your own point of view, presenting an argument in standard form for your conclusion.

Exercises

1. Write a dialogue between Ernesto and Brianna. Ernesto argues that nothing comes of what humans do. Brianna argues that humans have accomplished many things of lasting value.
2. Construct a thought experiment to test the claim that it is impossible for anyone other than God to live up to an ideal.

Activities

1. Watch the movie *Fight Club*, directed by David Fincher (1999). Why does the main character feel his life is meaningless and what does he do about it?
2. Read Camus' novel, *The Stranger*. How does it illustrate the feeling of despair discussed in this chapter?
3. Research songs that deal with existential crisis and write a paper about them.
4. Write a poem about an existential crisis you have had.
5. Write a letter to yourself to open on your 40th birthday.

References

Camus, A. (1955). *The myth of Sisyphus and other essays* (J. O'Brien, Trans.). New York: Random House.

Kierkegaard, S. (1941). *Repetition* (W. Lowrie, Trans.). Princeton, NJ: Princeton University Press. (Original work published 1843)

Taylor, R. (2004). The meaning of life. In D. Benatar (Ed.), *Life, death, and meaning: Key philosophical readings on the big questions* (pp. 19–28). Lanham, MD: Rowman & Littlefield.

Further Reading

Blackford, R. (2003). Sisyphus and the meaning of life. *Quadrant, 47*(10), 54–8.

Cottingham, J. (2003). *On the meaning of life.* New York: Routledge.

Heinegg, P. (2003). *Mortalism: Readings on the meaning of life.* Amherst, NY: Prometheus Books.

Kernes, J. L., Kinnier, R., Tribbensee, N., & Van Puymbroeck, C. M. (2003). What eminent people have said about the meaning of life. *Journal of Humanistic Psychology, 43,* 105–129.

Levy, N. (2005). Downshifting and meaning in life. *Ratio, 18*(2), 176–189.

Metz, T. (2002). Recent work on the meaning of life. *Ethics, 112,* 781–815.

Ovadia, S. (2003). Suggestions of the postmodern self: Value changes in American high school students 1976–1999. *Sociological Perspectives, 46,* 239–256.

Thomson, G. (2003). *On the meaning of life.* London: Thomson/Wadsworth.

APPENDIX A
Dialogue Worksheet

Date: _____

Group Name: _____

Dialogue Length: _____

Dialogue Title: _____

Screen Writer: _____

Director: _____

Narrator: _____

Actors: (1) _____

             (2) _____

             (3) _____

             (4) _____

             (5) _____

Philosophical Question Raised by Dialogue: _____

_____

Comments/Feedback (to be filled out after performance): _____

_____

_____

_____

DIALOGUE OUTLINE

The Setting: _____

_____

_____

_____

_____

The Action: _____

_____

_____

_____

_____

The Point: _____

_____

_____

_____

_____

APPENDIX B
Logic Skills

Philosophers explore controversial ideas through argumentation. By making an argument for or against a view, we test the strength of our beliefs and discover new ideas. Making an argument is a skill. Just like any other skill, such as playing golf, painting a picture, or fixing a car, becoming good at it takes practice. Although there are no right or wrong positions in philosophy, some arguments are better than others.

Logic is the study of argumentation. Learning some basic principles of logic will enable you to evaluate the arguments of others and construct more effective arguments of your own.

I. Definitions

An *argument* is a set of statements consisting of at least two premises and at least one conclusion. The *conclusion* of the argument is a statement you are trying to prove. The *premises* are the reasons supporting the conclusion. A good argument is like a mathematical equation because the premises "add up" to the conclusion in the same way that one plus one equals two. When you encounter an argument in real life, it is likely to be written out in a paragraph or spoken in conversation. Because it can be difficult to evaluate arguments in these forms, philosophers rewrite them in *standard form*. In standard form, you number each step and draw a line before the conclusion as follows:

1. Socrates is a man.   (premise)
2. All men are mortal.   (premise)

---

3. Therefore, Socrates is mortal.   (conclusion)

There are two basic criteria for evaluating arguments, namely, validity and soundness. People often use the terms *valid* and *sound* interchangeably for any old idea that they happen to like. But, in philosophy, these terms have technical definitions.

Validity concerns the structure of the argument. An argument is valid when the premises guarantee the conclusion. Consider the following analogy. Suppose you find a house you would like to buy. First, you should examine its structure. Will the floors and walls hold? You would not want to buy a house that will fall down when you step inside! Validity is an objective judgment, meaning that it is a matter of fact, not a matter of opinion. You can test the validity of an argument by asking yourself the following question: If the premises were true, would the conclusion have to be true? Notice that, for validity, it is not relevant whether or not the premises are actually true. This is because validity concerns structure rather than content of the argument.

Soundness concerns the content of the argument. An argument is sound under two conditions: (1) it is valid, and (2) the premises are true. Go back to our analogy. After you determine that the floor and the walls of the house will hold, you can walk around inside and check out the furnishings. Does it come with your favorite kitchen appliances? Is it fully carpeted? Are the walls painted nice colors? The more you like its contents, the more likely you are to buy the house. Because premises are always subject to revision, soundness is usually a subjective judgment. There is no objective test for soundness as there is for validity. But, you can use reasons and evidence to show why you accept or reject the content.

Although few arguments are perfect, some are better than others. An invalid argument is the worst of all. If an argument is invalid, then you have to start over. (When the floors and walls of your house will not hold, the best thing to do is tear it down and rebuild.) When an argument is valid, we say that the premises *imply* the conclusion, or that the conclusion *follows from* the premises. This means that the structure will hold, and someone might accept it as sound. (When a house has a solid structure and some furnishings, someone might buy it even if you decide not to.) A sound argument is the best. Don't call an argument sound unless you believe its premises are true. If you call an argument sound, that means you're buying it!

Validity and soundness seem simple enough, but they can be tricky. The following exercises will help you learn them correctly.

Exercises, Set 1

Put each of the following arguments into standard form. Then, tell whether or not it is valid, and why.

1. The best restaurant is in Cleveland. Cleveland is in Ohio. Therefore, the best restaurant is in Ohio.
2. Ohio is in the United States. The best theme park is in the United States. Therefore, Canada is not in the United States.
3. The best theme park is not in the United States. Canada is not in the United States. Therefore, the best theme park is in Canada.
4. The best restaurant is in Cleveland. Cleveland is in Canada. Therefore, the best restaurant is in Canada.
5. Because the best restaurant is in Cleveland and Cleveland is in Ohio, the best restaurant is in Ohio.
6. The best restaurant is obviously not in Canada. After all, the best restaurant is in Ohio, and Ohio is not in Canada.
7. The best restaurant is in Cleveland, and Ohio is in the United States. Therefore, the best restaurant is in the United States.
8. Cleveland is in the United States because Ohio is in the United States, and Cleveland is in Ohio.
9. George Washington was a founding father of the United States. George Washington was the first president of the United States. Therefore, the first president of the United States was also a founding father.
10. On Earth, all baseballs will fall when dropped. George let go of his baseball at the top of the tower. The ball fell.
11. Are any of the above arguments sound in your view? Which one(s) cannot be sound?

II. Paradigm Standard Forms

Philosophers have identified a number of paradigm standard forms and given them names. It is useful to know these paradigms so that you can recognize them when you see them or hear them used in an argument. When an argument is structured in accordance with any of these paradigms it is always valid. The paradigms can also be used in combination to make more sophisticated arguments. Philosophers use symbols to abbreviate these paradigms as follows.

Modus Ponens

1. If the cookies are golden brown, then they are finished baking.
2. The cookies are golden brown.
   _____
3. Therefore, the cookies are finished baking.

$$P \rightarrow Q$$
$$P$$
_____
$$Q$$

Modus Tollens

1. If the cookies were golden brown, then they would be finished baking.
2. But, the cookies are not finished baking.
   _____
3. Therefore, the cookies are not golden brown.

$$P \rightarrow Q$$
$$\sim Q$$
_____
$$\sim P$$

Modus ponens and modus tollens are built out of "If . . . then" statements called *conditional statements*. The "if" part of a conditional statement is called the *antecedent*. The "then" part of a conditional statement is called the *consequent*.

Before proceeding, you should take note of two common errors. Although the following standard forms look somewhat like modus ponens and modus tollens, they are invalid:

$$P \rightarrow Q$$
$$Q$$
_____
$$P$$

$$P \rightarrow Q$$
$$\sim P$$
_____
$$\sim Q$$

The first is called the *fallacy of denying the antecedent* while the second is called the fallacy of *affirming the consequent*. Plug in content of your own to see why the inferences are unwarranted.

Hypothetical Syllogism

1. If Jin comes to the party, then Chris will come to the party.
2. If Chris comes to the party, then Pat will come to the party.
   _____
3. Therefore, if Jin comes to the party, then Pat will come to the party

$$P \rightarrow Q$$
$$Q \rightarrow R$$
$$\overline{\qquad\qquad}$$
$$P \rightarrow R$$

Chain Reasoning

1. Nellie is a dog.
2. A dog is a mammal.
   _____
3. Nellie is a mammal.

$$P \, \varepsilon \, Q$$
$$Q \, \varepsilon \, R$$
$$\overline{\qquad\qquad}$$
$$P \, \varepsilon \, R$$

Disjunctive Syllogism

1. Either the butler did it or the maid did it.
2. The butler did not do it.
   _____
3. Therefore, the maid did it.

$$P \, \omega \, Q$$
$$\sim P$$
$$\overline{\qquad\qquad}$$
$$Q$$

Exercises, Set 2

Symbolize each of the following arguments in standard form and name the paradigm. Note that, as in real life, the statements may not be given to you in the correct order, there may be extra sentences that do not belong in the standard form, and there may even be some statements missing.

1. You are such a jerk. If you had left enough gas in the car, then we would have made it to the gas station. But, we did not make it to the gas station. You therefore failed to leave enough gas in the car. (P = enough gas in the car; Q = make it to the gas station)
2. I want you either to be quiet or leave. Because you obviously cannot be quiet, you will have to leave. (P = be quiet; Q = leave)

3. Hmmm. What should I order? If they allow you to substitute a salad for the potato, then I will order the fish plate. Oh, it says right here, they do allow you to substitute. So, I will order the fish plate.

4. Your friend Sammy is one of the students who lives in the dorms, right? Well, here's what happened. All the students who live in the dorms ate in the cafeteria, and everyone who ate at the cafeteria got food poisoning. We took everyone who got food poisoning to the hospital. So, yes, I believe Sammy is in the hospital. (P = Sammy; Q = student who lives in the dorms; R = ate in the cafeteria; S = got food poisoning; T = ended up in the hospital)

5. If I had bombed the last test, I would need to study for tomorrow's test. But I didn't bomb the last test. Hence, I do not need to study for tomorrow's test.

6. Alfred, you give massages as often as possible because you really love it and when you really love something, you do it often as you can. (P = you love to give massages; Q = you give massages as often as possible)

7. Don't touch that switch! If the light doesn't come on, it could be dangerous. You see, if the light doesn't come on, then the wiring is faulty and if the wiring is faulty, then there is an electrical current in the switch. And, believe me, if there is an electrical current in the switch, it could be dangerous. (P = the light comes on; Q = the wiring is faulty; R = there is an electrical current in the switch, S = it could be dangerous.)

8. Tron would not have burned a copy of this remix album if it were not better than the original. Because Tron did burn a copy, it must be better. But, this remix album is better only if the original is terrible. (P = The remix album is better than the original; Q = Tron burns a copy; R = The original is terrible.)

9. I work all the time because I need money. Money is freedom because it enables me to do what I want. Without money, I have to rely on other people too much. I don't want to rely on other people too much because freedom is happiness. Talk to someone who has lived in prison, and they will tell you that nothing is better than being free. I'm not an idiot. I just want what everyone wants, which is happiness. That's why everyone works all the time, because, in the end, money is what everybody wants. And, if money is what everybody wants, then I'm going to work as much as I can. (P = money; Q = freedom; R =

happiness; S = what everyone wants, T = I'm going to work as much as I can)

10. I'm telling you, it's true. Dating is like cooking. It requires good timing and good taste. But, if dating is like cooking, then it's a skill, and if it's a skill, people should not assume they do not need training. I mean, most people who really cook learn how to do it from their parents while growing up, or they take some classes, or they read a book about it. Now, you're not going to be able to learn dating from your parents or in a class. So, get a book. (P = dating requires good timing and good taste Q = dating is like cooking; R = dating is a skill; S = people need training in dating; T = you should learn from your parents; U = you should learn by taking classes; V = you should learn by reading a book)

APPENDIX C
Answer Key

Exercises, Set 1

1.

1. The best restaurant is in Cleveland.
2. Cleveland is in Ohio.

___

3. Therefore, the best restaurant is in Ohio.

This argument is valid because the conclusion follows from the premises. (For validity, it does not matter whether or not you agree with the statements.)

2.

1. Ohio is in the United States.
2. The best theme park is in United States.

___

3. Therefore, Canada is not in the United States.

This argument is invalid because the conclusion does not follow from the premises. (It does not matter whether or not the statements are true.)

3.

1. The best theme park is not in the United States.
2. Canada is not in the United States.

---

3. Therefore, the best theme park is in Canada.

This argument is invalid because the premises do not imply the conclusion. (The best theme park might be in some country other than the United States or Canada.)

4.

1. The best restaurant is in Cleveland.
2. Cleveland is in Canada.

---

3. Therefore, the best restaurant is in Canada.

This argument is valid because the premises imply the conclusion. (It is irrelevant that premise 2 is definitely false.)

5.

1. The best restaurant is in Cleveland.
2. Cleveland is in Ohio.

---

3. Therefore, the best restaurant is in Ohio.

This argument is valid because the premises guarantee the conclusion. (Watch for words such as "since," "because," and "due to," to indicate premises and words such as "so," "therefore," and "hence" to indicate conclusions.)

6.

1.   The best restaurant is in Ohio.
2.   Ohio is not in Canada.

_____

3.   Therefore, the best restaurant is not in Canada.

This argument is valid because the conclusion is implied by the premises. (In this case, the conclusion is mentioned first. Use context to distinguish premises from conclusions.)

7.

1.   The best restaurant is in Cleveland.
2.   Ohio is in the United States.

_____

3.   Therefore, the best restaurant is in the United States.

This argument is invalid because the inference is unwarranted. (The premises do not give you any information about the relationship between Cleveland and Ohio. What premise could you add to this argument make it valid?)

8.

1.   Cleveland is in Ohio.
2.   Ohio is in the United States.

_____

3.   Therefore, Cleveland is in the United States.

This argument is valid because the inference is warranted. (For standard form, you should always put the steps in the order that is easiest to read.)

9.

1. George Washington was a founding father of the United States.
2. George Washington was the first president of the United States.

3. Therefore, the first president of the United States was also a founding father.

This argument is valid.

10.

1. On Earth, all baseballs will fall when dropped.
2. George let go of his baseball at the top of the tower.

3. The ball fell.

This argument is valid.

11.

Arguments 1, 5, and 6 could be sound, depending on your opinion about best restaurants and theme parks. Argument 9 is almost certainly sound, unless we have our history wrong, and 10 will be regarded as sound provided you have good evidence that George really did drop the ball. Arguments 2, 3, and 7 cannot be sound because they are not valid. Even though Argument 4 is valid, it is unsound, assuming that "Cleveland" refers to the city that is in Ohio. Argument 8 is definitely sound. Although soundness is usually a matter of opinion, some arguments are definitely sound or unsound.

EXERCISE SET TWO

1. Modus Tollens

1. If you had left enough gas in the car, then we would have made it to the gas station.
2. We did not make it to the gas station.

---

3. Therefore, you did not leave enough gas in the car.

1. P → Q
2. ~Q
3. ~P

This standard form leaves out the opening insult, which is irrelevant to the argument.

2. Disjunctive Syllogism

1. Either you must be quiet or you must leave.
2. You cannot be quiet.

---

3. Therefore, you must leave.

1. P ω Q
2. ~P
3. Q

This standard form rephrases some of the original language for greater precision. Also note that there is no limit to the number of disjuncts in a disjunctive syllogism. For example, this argument could have said: "either read quietly, take a nap, or leave," and then eliminated the first two possibilities.

3. Modus Ponens

1. If they allow you to substitute a salad for the potato, then I will order the fish plate.
2. They do allow you to substitute a salad for the potato.

3. Therefore, I will order the fish plate.

1. P → Q
2. P
————
3. Q

This standard form leaves out the opening question, which is irrelevant to the argument.

4. Chain Reasoning

1. Sammy is a dorm student.
2. Dorm students eat in the cafeteria.
3. Those who ate in the cafeteria got food poisoning.
4. The people who got food poisoning are in the hospital.

5. Therefore, Sammy is in the hospital.

1. P ε Q
2. Q ε R
3. R ε S
4. S ε T
————
5. P ε T

This standard form changes the opening question into a statement that is relevant to the argument. It leaves out the second sentence, which is irrelevant, and interprets the argument as building a set of sets. There is no limit to the number of steps you can add in chain reasoning or hypothetical syllogism.

5. Not a Paradigm: Fallacy of Denying the Antecedent

1. If I bombed the last test, then I would need to study for tomorrow's test.
2. I did not bomb the last test.

1. P → Q
2. ~P
————
3. ~Q

3. Therefore, I do not need to study for tomorrow's test.

This standard form is not valid because the premises do not guarantee the conclusion. If you think about it you will see why. There could be other reasons why you need to study. For example, suppose tomorrow's test is five times harder than the last one. Then, the fact that you didn't bomb the last test is irrelevant. Notice that we could produce a similar error as follows:

1. If I bombed the last test, then I need to study for tomorrow's test.
2. I need to study for tomorrow's test.
_____

3. Therefore, I must have bombed the last test

1. P → Q
2. Q
_____
3. P

This is the fallacy of affirming the consequent, and it is invalid. Again, the premises do not guarantee the conclusion because there may be other reasons why you need to study for tomorrow's test. Do not proceed until you clearly understand why denying the antecedent and affirming the consequent are fallacious forms of argument.

6. Modus Ponens

1. If you love to give massages, then you give massages as often as possible.
2. You love to give massages.
_____

3. Therefore, you give massages as often as possible.

1. P → Q
2. P
_____
3. Q

This standard form oversimplifies the argument, which actually makes a claim, not just about Alfred, but about people in general. The symbolization of general claims is studied in formal logic courses. Although we will mostly avoid this level of complexity, you may be interested to see how a more accurate symbolization would look:

Let x = all people
Let y = all activities
Let L = loves
Let D = does
Let a = Alfred
Let m = massage

<table>
<tr><td>1. For all people and for all activities, if a person loves an activity, then that person does that activity.</td><td>1. (x)(y)(xLy → xDy)</td></tr>
<tr><td>2. Alfred is a person</td><td>2. a ε x</td></tr>
<tr><td>3. Massage is an activity.</td><td>3. m ε y</td></tr>
<tr><td>4. Alfred loves massage.</td><td>4. aLm</td></tr>
<tr><td></td><td>5. aDm</td></tr>
</table>

5. Therefore, Alfredo does massage.

7. Hypothetical Syllogism

<table>
<tr><td>1. If the light does not come on, then the wiring is faulty.</td><td>1. ~P → Q</td></tr>
<tr><td>2. If the wiring is faulty, then there is an electrical current in the switch.</td><td>2. Q → R</td></tr>
<tr><td>3. If there is an electrical current in the switch, then it could be dangerous.</td><td>3. R → S</td></tr>
<tr><td></td><td>4. ~P → S</td></tr>
</table>

4. Therefore, if the light does not come on, then it could be dangerous.

This standard form leaves out the command at the beginning of the paragraph. Suppose we discovered that the light does not in fact come on. We could then make the command into the conclusion by adding the symbol "T" for "you should not touch the switch" along with the implied premise. (If it could be dangerous, then you should not touch the switch.) This would result in an extended argument that combines modus ponens with hypothetical syllogism as follows:

1. The light does not come on.
2. If the light doesn't come on, then the wiring is faulty.
3. If the wiring is faulty, then there is an electrical current in the switch.
4. If there is an electrical current in the switch, then it could be dangerous.
5. If the switch could be dangerous, then you should not touch it.

1. ~P
2. ~P → Q
3. Q → R
4. R → S
5. S → T
———
6. T

6. Therefore, you should not touch the switch.

8. Modus Tollens and Modus Ponens

1. If this remix album was not better than the original, then Tron would not have burned a copy.
2. Tron burned a copy of the remix album.

3. The remix album must be better than the original.
4. If the remix album is better, then the original is terrible.

1. ~P → ~Q
———
2. Q
3. P
4. P → R
———
5. R

(5. The original is terrible.)

The opening conditional statement in this argument presents the antecedent before the consequent. Don't let this common variation confuse you. The phrase that is attached to "if" is always the antecedent. Although Step 2 affirms Q, this is not the fallacy of affirming the consequent because the consequent is ~Q. The second conditional uses the operator "only if." The phrase attached to "only if" is always the consequent. The author of the argument did not bother to state the final conclusion of the argument so we have supplied it.

9. Chain Reasoning and Modus Ponens

1. Money is freedom.
2. Freedom is happiness.
3. Happiness is what everybody wants.

---

4. So, money is what everybody wants.
5. If money is what everybody wants, then I'm going to work as much as I can.

---

6. Therefore, I'm going to work as much as I can.

1. P ε Q
2. Q ε R
3. R ε S
---
4. P ε S
5. (PεS) → T
---
6. T

This is a "double-decker" standard form. On the first deck, it uses chain reasoning to show that a number of different things are actually the same thing. On the second deck, it uses the conclusion of the first deck to draw a second conclusion. We call Step 4 a "subconclusion" and tag it with the word "so" rather than "therefore."

10. Modus Ponens, Hypothetical Syllogism, and Disjunctive Syllogism

1. (If dating requires good timing and good taste, then it is like cooking.)
2. Dating requires good timing and good taste.

---

3. So, dating is like cooking.
4. If dating is like cooking, then it is a skill.
5. If dating is a skill, then it is not true that you do not need training.
6. ("It is not true that you do not need training" means "you need training.")

1. P → Q
2. P
---
3. Q
4. Q → R
5. R → ~~S
6. ~~S = S
7. S → T ω U ω V
8. ~T
9. ~U
---
10. V

7. (If you need training, then you should learn either from parents, or from taking a class, or from reading a book.)
8. You should not learn from parents.
9. You should not learn from taking a class.

___

10. Therefore, you should learn from reading a book.

This argument implies three hidden premises, indicated in the standard form with parentheses. Philosophers read arguments charitably. This means they try to interpret each argument in the best possible light, whether they agree with it or not. Rather than accuse this author of presenting an invalid argument, we can easily supply the missing steps. Step 6 is called "double negation."

GLOSSARY

altruism: view that one should help other people even at a cost to oneself

continuity theory: view that each person is one continuous thing throughout life

creation ex nihilo: view that the universe was created out of nothing

creationism: view that only God could create a mechanistic system as complex and beautiful as Earth and its inhabitants

cyclicism: view that the universe goes through endless cycles, the constant companion of time

determinism: view that everything we do is determined by desires stemming from our biological makeup or our environment

dualism: view that a human being is two things: a mind and a body

empiricism: view that sense experience is our one and only source of information about the world

ethical egoism: view that the world would be a better place if everyone always acted to benefit him- or herself

evolution: view that all life on our planet developed from basic chemical ingredients over a period of millions and millions of years

existentialism: preoccupation with the meaning of life

externalism: view that the meaning of language lies in its use

falsification: try to show that a theory doesn't fit facts, prove a theory false

fideism: from Latin word **faith**; belief in God even though there isn't sufficient evidence of his existence

idealism: view that asserts that only ideas exist

internalism: view that the meaning of language lies in the thoughts it stands for

libertarianism: view that human beings are at liberty to make free choices

materialism: view that physical matter is the only thing that exists; all our thoughts can be explained in purely physical terms

metaphysics: beyond the study of nature

moral objectivism: view that there are universal moral truths, even though we may not always know what they are, and may not always agree about them

moral relativism: view that right and wrong both depend on the person—there are no universal moral truths

physics: scientific study of nature

psychology: scientific study of the workings of the human mind

rationalism: view that we can learn important things about the world by examining the contents if our own minds, and that we can use reason alone to gain scientific knowledge of the future

scientific realism: view that while our senses sometimes deceive us, science can give us reliable knowledge about the world

strong AI: view that asserts that computers can possess consciousness

succession theory: view that each person is a succession of beings throughout life

verification: confirmation of a theory by experience or experiment

voluntarism: view that sometimes you are justified in believing in something because you want to believe that thing

weak AI: view that while we may learn important things about thinking by comparing and contrasting thinking with what computers do, machines cannot think.

ABOUT THE AUTHORS

For the past several years, Sharon Kaye and Paul Thomson have been teaching philosophy to secondary school students through the Carroll-Cleveland Philosophers' Program, which won the 2006 American Philosophical Association Award for Excellence and Innovation in Philosophy Programs. This textbook grew out of their experience with the Carroll-Cleveland Philosophers' Program. The authors have presented the drama pedagogy employed in the book at academic conferences in Chicago; San Francisco; Manchester College, Oxford; New College, Cambridge; New College, Oxford; Toronto; and at the University of Strathclyde in Glasgow, Scotland.

Sharon Kaye received her Ph.D. from the University of Toronto in 1997. She currently serves as an associate professor at John Carroll University, teaching philosophy of education, philosophy of friendship, metaphysics, and medieval philosophy, among other courses. She has published widely on various topics including *On Augustine*, with Paul Thomson. She is also the faculty advisor for the campus chapter of Amnesty international.

Paul Thomson received his Ph.D. from Princeton University in 1990, and served as assistant and associate professor at John Carroll University until the beginning of 2007, teaching and publishing in epistemology, philosophy of science, and early modern philosophy. He is also past director of John Carroll's First Year Seminar. He now serves as Philosopher-in-Residence at Columbia Secondary School, a magnet school in mathematics, science, and engineering formed as a partnership between the New York City Department of Education and Columbia University. A philosophy course at each grade level will be an integral and mandatory part of the school's curriculum.